OLD TESTAMENT GUIDES

General Editor
R.N. Whybray

ISAIAH 1–39

ISAIAH 1–39

J. Barton

Sheffield Academic Press

Copyright © 1995 Sheffield Academic Press

Published by Sheffield Academic Press Ltd
Mansion House
19 Kingfield Road
Sheffield, S11 9AS
England

Printed on acid-free paper in Great Britain
by The Cromwell Press
Melksham, Wiltshire

British Library Cataloguing in Publication Data

A catalogue record for this book is available
from the British Library

ISBN 1-85075-541-8

Contents

List of Abbreviations

ABD	*Anchor Bible Dictionary*, ed. D.N. Freedman, G.A. Herion, D.F. Graf, and J.D. Pleins
ANET	J.B. Pritchard (ed.), *Ancient Near Eastern Texts*, 3rd edn, Princeton: Princeton University Press, 1969
BEvT	Beiträge zur Evangelischen Theologie
BETL	Bibliotheca ephemeridum theologicarum lovaniensium
BWANT	Beiträge zur Wissenschaft vom Alten und Neuen Testament
BZAW	Beihefte zur *Zeitschrift für die Alttestamentliche Wissenschaft*
CBQ	*Catholic Biblical Quarterly*
ConBOT	Coniectanea biblica, Old Testament
EB	Etudes bibliques
EvTh	*Evangelische Theologie*
IB	*Interpreter's Bible*
ICC	International Critical Commentary
Int	*Interpretation*
JBL	*Journal of Biblical Literature*
JEA	*Journal of Egyptian Archaeology*
JSOT	*Journal for the Study of the Old Testament*
JSOTSup	*Journal for the Study of the Old Testament, Supplement Series*
JTS	*Journal of Theological Studies*
NCB	New Century Bible
OTL	Old Testament Library
OTS	*Oudtestamentische Studiën*
SBL	Society of Biblical Literature
SBLDS	SBL Dissertation Series
SBLSP	SBL Seminar Papers
SBS	Stuttgarter Bibelstudien

SBT	Studies in Biblical Theology
SJT	*Scottish Journal of Theology*
TLZ	*Theologische Literaturzeitung*
VT	*Vetus Testamentum*
VTSup	Supplements to *Vetus Testamentum*
WBC	Word Biblical Commentary
WMANT	Wissenschaftliche Monographien zum Alten und Neuen Testament
ZAW	*Zeitschrift für die alttestamentliche Wissenschaft*

Introduction

Isaiah is one of the most difficult of the prophet books, but also one of the most rewarding. Sometimes the reader feels that there is a dense forest to beat a way through before there is any chance of meeting the prophet, and the form a commentary is bound to take tends to reinforce this feeling: each verse has to be held up against the light, evaluated, and then laid by until the moment comes for a judgment on the whole book. And sometimes this moment never seems to arrive.

The conviction behind this study guide is that things are not as bad as they seem. The book of Isaiah, and even the first thirty-nine chapters which are the subject of this book, is indeed complex. But it is also distinctive: there are very few passages which might just as well come from any other prophet. It was put together by many hands, yet it is far from being a mere rubbish-tip, the insides of many unconnected filing-cabinets. Its core is the words of Isaiah, son of Amoz, a far from shadowy figure, and one of the sharpest intellects among ancient Israel's not inconsiderable thinkers. Reconstructing his thought is not easy, nearly three thousand years later, but neither is it impossible. The book that bears his name enables us to see how the themes of his teaching were both taken seriously and yet modified, subtly or drastically, over the succeeding centuries.

The study of Isaiah has passed through three main phases in modern times. The great and liberating discovery of nineteenth-century scholarship was that the book was not the product of one confused mind, but of a number of perfectly clear ones. At least three 'Isaiahs' had contributed to it, their work being found respectively in 1–39, 40–55 and 56–66. Further study revealed that 'First Isaiah' (1–39) was itself a composite work containing material that might span a number of centuries. The precise focus on each writer, in his own historical setting, which this made possible is the abiding legacy of 'historical-critical' scholarship, and I have assumed that anyone beginning to study Isaiah will want to know about it, even though it has its detractors nowadays.

Once the materials out of which the book is made had been identified, however, attention shifted to the process by which they were assembled, and the intentions of those who assembled them—the editors or 'redactors'. What an editor in (say) the sixth century BC was trying to tell his readers, by the way he put together Isaianic and post-Isaianic oracles, is just as interesting as the original message of the prophet himself. If there was once a tendency to consign passages deemed 'secondary' to the wastepaper basket, since the 1950s scholars have shown a great interest in these post-Isaianic compilers, who were often powerful thinkers and theologians in their own right.

Thirdly, the last two decades have seen the rise of an interest in reading Isaiah just as it is, in the way we normally read literary works, emphasizing the unity and coherence which the book does possess, for all its complicated history. The impulse for such a 'holistic' reading may be strictly literary, or it may be religious—arguing that what Holy Scripture contains is the whole book of Isaiah, not its hypothetical earlier components, and therefore it is as a whole that we are meant to read it.

There is often some hostility between supporters of holistic reading and those wedded to historical criticism, and it is as well for the reader to be aware of this. But all the approaches outlined are intellectually serious, committed to careful engagement with the text, and productive of rich insights. A study guide intended for people in the 1990s is bound to introduce all of them, and to invite the reader to give them all a fair hearing.

This is not to say that what is presented here is a neutral account of Isaiah 1–39 that everyone can agree with. Naturally my own concerns and interests emerge, both in the content of the different chapters and in the manner and order in which the material is presented. Each chapter ends, as is usual in this series, with suggestions for further reading. Books and articles accessible to beginners are asterisked. I have concentrated on works in English, but Old Testament studies is an area in which German is still a major language of scholarship, and a number of German (and a few French) resources are listed for those who can make use of them.

Biblical quotations come from the Revised Standard Version (RSV). There are a few places in Isaiah where verse numbering differs between the Hebrew text and English translations, and in these cases I have followed the English numbering. Anyone wanting to refer to the Hebrew will find that the RSV clearly alerts the reader to the discrepancy.

Further Reading

General guides to the prophets

*J. Blenkinsopp, *A History of Prophecy in Israel: From the Settlement in the Land to the Hellenistic Period* (London: SPCK, 1984); on Isaiah, pp. 106-18; the best modern work on prophecy as a whole.

E.W. Heaton, *The Old Testament Prophets* (London: Darton, Longman & Todd, 2nd edn, 1977 [1958]); still a valuable introduction to the subject.

*J.F.A. Sawyer, *Prophecy and the Prophets of the Old Testament* (Oxford: Oxford University Press, 1987; 2nd edn *Prophecy and the Biblical Prophets*, 1993); a readable, up-to-date guide.

*J. Lindblom, *Prophecy in Ancient Israel* (Oxford: Blackwell, 1962); dated but still useful, especially on the composition of the prophetic books.

G. von Rad, *Old Testament Theology*, II (Edinburgh: Oliver & Boyd, 1965).

W. McKane, 'Prophecy and the Prophetic Literature', in *Tradition and Interpretation* (ed. G.W. Anderson; Oxford: Clarendon Press, 1979), pp. 163-88.

Israel's Prophetic Tradition: Essays in Honour of Peter R. Ackroyd (ed. R. Coggins, A. Phillips and M. Knibb; Cambridge: Cambridge University Press, 1982).

General works on Isaiah

A.G. Auld, 'Poetry, Prophecy, Hermeneutic: Recent Studies in Isaiah', *SJT* 33 (1980), pp. 567-81.

M.A. Sweeney, 'The Book of Isaiah in Recent Research', *Currents in Research: Biblical Studies* 1 (1993), pp. 141-62.

The Book of Isaiah (ed. J. Vermeylen; BETL 81; Leuven: Leuven University Press, 1989); a collection of essays on Isaiah.

R. Kilian, *Jesaja 1–39* (Erträge der Forschung, 200; Darmstadt, 1983).

Commentaries in English

*R.E. Clements, *Isaiah 1–39* (NCB; Grand Rapids: Eerdmans; London: Marshall, Morgan & Scott, 1980); probably the most useful current commentary on the English text, balanced and straightforward.

O. Kaiser, *Isaiah 1–12 and Isaiah 13–39* (OTL; London: SCM Press, 1972, 1974 (second edns 1983—completely revised); useful medium-length commentary, sceptical of finding any of Isaiah's own words in 1–39.

H. Wildberger, *Isaiah 1–12: A Commentary* (Minneapolis: Fortress Press, 1991); the other two volumes of Wildberger's commentary are not yet translated.

*R.B.Y. Scott, 'The Book of Isaiah, 1–39', in *IB*, V, pp. 149-381.

G.B. Gray, *Isaiah I–XXVII* (ICC; Edinburgh: T. & T. Clark, 1912); still a classic, with much useful detailed information. Gray did not live to complete the remaining chapters.

*A.S. Herbert, *The Book of the Prophet Isaiah 1–39* (Cambridge Commentary on the New English Bible; Cambridge: Cambridge University Press, 1973); good simple commentary.

Commentaries in German

H. Wildberger, *Jesaja 1–12* (see above for translation), Jesaja 13–27, *Jesaja 28–39* (Biblischer Kommentar; Neukirchen–Vluyn: Neukirchener Verlag, 1965–72, 1974–78, 1978–82).

B. Duhm, *Das Buch Jesaja* (Handkommentar zum Alten Testament: Göttingen, 1868 [repr. 1922]; historically probably the most important commentary on Isaiah.

1

THE PROPHET AND THE BOOK

The prophet Isaiah lived in Jerusalem in the eighth century
BC, some time between 750 and 700, and prophesied during
the reigns of Jotham, Ahaz and Hezekiah—perhaps also
under Jotham's predecessor Uzziah, as the first verse of the
book claims (see Milgrom). The book that bears his name was
to become one of the most important in the prophetic collection. In Judaism it supplies nearly half the readings from the
prophets in the synagogue liturgy. Its importance in
Christianity can be seen from the New Testament, where no
other prophetic book is quoted anything like so often. For the
earliest Christians it formed, together with Genesis and the
Psalms, the effective core of the Old Testament.

But the relation between the prophet and his book is one of
the most vexed questions in biblical studies. There is such
widespread agreement that chs. 40–66 are the work of a later
prophet or prophets that this will not be discussed here at
all—'Second' and 'Third Isaiah' (Isa. 40–55 and 56–66) are
the subject of other volumes in this series. (How the three
collections came to be formed into one book, and what 'message' if any that book conveys as a finished product, will be
discussed below (in Chapter 6), since this is one of the current focal points in the study of the book of Isaiah).

But the removal of chs. 40–66 does not mean that in chs.
1–39 all is plain sailing. The vast majority of commentators
agree that by no means everything in these chapters can
derive from the prophet Isaiah himself, because there are
passages—sometimes extensive ones—that refer to periods

later than that of his prophetic activity. It is usual in biblical study to refer to passages that do go back to the prophet as 'authentic' or 'genuine', and to those that do not as 'inauthentic' or 'secondary'. As we shall see, these terms must not be taken as expressing value judgments, only historical hypotheses about who wrote which parts of the prophetic books. But in none of the prophets is the question of 'authenticity' so difficult as in Isaiah. Scholars have spent a great deal of time—some may think, an inordinate amount of time—in trying to solve it.

On a superficial level a survey of what commentators have said about this question can in fact induce despair, or perhaps exasperation, that there is so little agreement. The two extremes are represented by the recent work of J.H. Hayes and P. Irvine, who hold that everything in 1–39 except for 34–35 and the stories in 36–39 goes back to the prophet Isaiah himself, and O. Kaiser's commentary, whose starting point is that there is no *prima facie* reason for thinking anything in the book 'genuine', and which in fact treats only a few core passages as Isaianic.

But there are many positions between these. Clements, for example, sees a large Isaianic core, but thinks this was expanded at subsequent points, especially through a major redaction in the time of Josiah (broadly following Hermann Barth). However, he treats as authentic passages such as the 'messianic' oracle of 9.2-7, which a commentator such as Kaiser would regard as almost self-evidently a later addition. Wildberger is considerably more conservative than this, though without approaching the root-and-branch avoidance of thinking any passages inauthentic that is to be found in Hayes and Irvine. But he does, for example think that 2.2-4 is by Isaiah, where many commentators regard it as a late insertion into the book (it also occurs in Micah [4.1-4] with only minor variations). This, with 9.2-7, tends to be quite an accurate indicator of commentators' attitudes towards questions of authenticity. Thinking these passages Isaianic often goes with a rather conservative attitude, a feeling that what is in Isaiah 1–39 should be thought of as deriving from Isaiah unless there are good reasons to the contrary. Those who think such oracles inauthentic often regard the Isaianic origin of the book's contents as an open question, to be decided on the merits of each case and with no 'benefit of the doubt' being given. Often this difference correlates with the difference between thinking that it *matters* (theologically) that Isaiah wrote at least substantial parts of the book that bears his name, and thinking, non-committally, that it is simply an interesting question whether he did or not.

Partly, then, for such theological reasons, and partly because of the diversity that is bound to prevail in any enquiry as complex as this, commentators differ very widely about authenticity. Anyone approaching the critical study of Isaiah 1–39 for the first time is likely to feel that almost any verse could be by almost anyone and come from almost any period. This can be discouraging.

But there is really more agreement between commentators than this may suggest. While there is probably nothing in the book on which all scholars agree, the overall picture is far from chaotic. Most disagreements are about matters of detail, and there is a considerable consensus on many aspects of the book and its authorship. We may consider this under four headings.

The Shape of the Book

There is fairly general agreement on how best to divide up Isaiah 1–39. Of some prophetic books commentators disagree widely about where one section ends and the next begins, and even about how larger sections are to be broken down into individual oracles. This is particularly noticeable, for example, in the study of Hosea. But in the case of Isaiah there is broad agreement at least about the main blocks of material, and quite a wide consensus even about the smaller units within these blocks. As Willis shows, a certain amount depends on just what constitutes a 'block' (or section, or pericope)—the more minutely we subdivide, the more room there is for disagreement. But so long as we use a broad brush, the following basic outline (which is close to the analysis in the commentary by R.B.Y. Scott) would not be very contentious.

1   *Introductory Collection of Oracles from Various Periods*

2–12   *Oracles about Judah and Jerusalem*

   2–5   Oracles of judgment and salvation
   6–8   The call of Isaiah and his prophecies in the time of the
          Syro–Ephraimite coalition
   9–11   Oracles about the Assyrians
   12   A psalm celebrating deliverance

13–23   *Oracles against Foreign Nations*

   13–14   Oracles about Babylon
   15–16   Oracles about Moab
   17   Oracles about Damascus
   18–19   Oracles about Egypt
   20   Narratives about Isaiah and his oracles concerning
          Egypt
   21   Oracles about Babylon
   22   Oracles in the time of the 'Assyrian crisis'
   23   Oracles about Tyre

24–27   *The 'Isaiah Apocalypse'*

          Oracles of judgment and salvation about an unidentified
          city

28–31   *Oracles Mainly about the 'Assyrian Crisis'*

   28   Oracles about the fate of Israel and Judah
   29   Oracles about the fate of Jerusalem
   30–31   Oracles about the anti-Assyrian alliance with Egypt

32–33   *Oracles about Human and Divine Kingship*

34–35   *Oracles of Judgment on Edom and Salvation for Israel*

36–39   *Narratives about Isaiah*

   36–37   The history of the 'Assyrian crisis'
   38–39   An account of Hezekiah's illness, his prayer and his
          alliance with Babylon

Some of the divisions are clearly marked in the text.
Chapter 2, for example, begins with a title 'The word which
Isaiah son of Amoz saw concerning Judah and Jerusalem'.
There are formal similarities between the parts of some
sections, with chs. 13–23 consisting of a series of poems
beginning 'The oracle concerning...', and oracles in chs.

28–31 beginning 'Woe...' And (though this is a little more subjective) there is a strong unity of style in, for example, chs. 24–27, which sets them off from the rest of the book. In principle this division, or something like it, might be agreed to equally by a reader who thought everything in the book came from Isaiah, or by one who thought that nothing did. But in practice it does tend to provide an agreed framework within which reasoned decisions can be made about where authentic material is to be found.

Secondary Material

Without ruling out the possibility of genuine oracles of Isaiah in any part of the book, there is widespread agreement that some sections are not very likely to contain much that goes back to the prophet:

(a) Chapters 24–27 are usually called 'the Isaiah Apocalypse'. This is because they are thought to resemble the 'apocalyptic' works common from about the third century BC onwards, represented in the biblical canon only by Daniel and Revelation, and perhaps also in sections of Joel and Zechariah. If it is true that apocalyptic came into being long after the Exile, and that these chapters of Isaiah belong to that genre, then obviously they cannot come from Isaiah himself. Not all commentators agree about this, but it is a widely held opinion.

(b) Chapters 36–38 are almost identical with 2 Kings 18–19, the account of the siege of Jerusalem by Sennacherib in 701 BC, though there are slight discrepancies. As with any such duplication of material in the Bible there are at least three possible explanations: Kings borrowed from Isaiah; Isaiah borrowed from Kings; both borrowed from a common source. Most (but not all) scholars think that the book of Isaiah took this section from Kings, which was probably written in the sixth century BC. In that case it clearly cannot go back to the prophet himself. In any case it should be noted that these chapters speak of Isaiah in the third person. People do sometimes write about themselves in the third person—Julius Caesar's memoirs of the Gallic Wars, for instance, say 'Caesar marshalled the army...Caesar advanced' and so on.

But it is probably simpler to explain these chapters as
the work of a historian. Of course they may still contain
historically accurate material *about* Isaiah, even though not
coming *from* him.

(c) The oracles against foreign nations in 13–23 are something of a rag-bag of material, probably from a number of
different periods. Some of them seem plainly to refer to
events later than the lifetime of Isaiah. This is clearest in the
case of the anti-Babylonian oracles (13–14). In the time of
Isaiah Babylon was not a major world power: the threat to
the small nations of Syria-Palestine came from the
Assyrians, whom the Babylonians would not overthrow and
replace until the late seventh century. On the assumption
that hostile oracles against Babylon presuppose a time at
which it was a danger to Judah, they cannot come from
Isaiah.

Against this it can be argued that the nations denounced
by the prophets were not always the current enemies of
Judah or Israel (this is true, for example of the oracles
against the nations in Amos 1–2), and that it is perfectly con-
ceivable that Isaiah could have foreseen the rise of Babylon
to take the place of Assyria as the oppressor of his people.
This could be argued either on the grounds of his superior
knowledge of the military situation (likely enough if he was
an official royal adviser, as some think), or on the grounds
that he received a divine revelation of the future beyond
what could have been known by natural means. The latter
argument wipes out all considerations of historical plausi-
bility, of course. But by the kinds of criterion we would use in
dating any other ancient document, the anti-Babylonian
oracles do not seem likely to be by Isaiah. When the rest of
Isaiah 13–23 is examined in the same way, only the material
about Egypt (18–19) seems to have a plausible context in
Isaiah's prophetic career—and some would think even that
doubtful.

(d) Chapters 34–35 form a rather puzzling section. Many
commentators treat it as a single unit: an oracle against the
Edomites, Israel's enemies, followed by a prophecy of the
glorious restoration of Israel itself. However, there is a wide
divergence in style between the two chapters. Chapter 34

talks of Yahweh's combat with the powers of evil in heaven, in a way perhaps even closer to apocalyptic literature than is the 'Isaiah Apocalypse' (see above). Chapter 34, on the other hand, is highly reminiscent of Isaiah 40–55—so much so that some think it is by Deutero-Isaiah, maybe even separated artificially from Isaiah 40 when 36–39 were inserted into the book. Arguments that bring 24–27 down into the post-exilic age have the same effect on 34, and the resemblance to Deutero-Isaiah makes it likely that 35 is no earlier than the sixth century. If the two chapters were combined before they became part of the book of Isaiah, they could form an extremely late addition—much later than Deutero- or Trito-Isaiah.

(e) Chapters 32–33 are a mysterious collection, rather neglected by commentators. Here arguments about dating and authenticity tend to become very subjective. For example, the oracle against the 'complacent women' in 32.9-14 can be compared with 3.16-26 (and with Amos 4.1-3), and pronounced appropriate to the mid-eighth century, when Isaiah's prophetic activity began (in the 740s or 730s). At this time the citizens of Jerusalem still felt untroubled by the threat of Assyria, and enjoyed life with no thought for the future. On the other hand, the continuation of the oracle in vv. 15-20 speaks of the outpouring of God's spirit in a way we associate with post-exilic hopes (cf. Joel 2.28-29). Perhaps a genuine oracle of Isaiah has been 'updated' by the addition of the prophecy about the spirit; or perhaps the whole chapter is a later addition.

The effect of considerations such as these is to leave us with a small core of passages in which the authentic message of the prophet Isaiah can reasonably be sought. The core consists primarily of Isaiah 1–12 and 28–31, though we must not ignore possible fragments of Isaianic material in other chapters, such as 18 and 32. This is not to say that everything in the core is authentic, only that there is probably little authentic material anywhere else.

It should be stressed again that the question of 'authenticity' is not primarily an evaluative question. It is not a judgment on the *quality* of the material in Isaiah 1–39, as though oracles judged 'inauthentic' were being thrown into the waste paper basket. It has to be admitted that commentators sometimes have conveyed this impression, but there has been a massive swing against such value judgments in the last twenty years or so. We shall look in Chapter 6 at the recent interest in reading Isaiah 1–39 (or indeed Isaiah 1–66) as a unified whole, in which all the components are of equal value. But to say that the inauthentic parts of the book are important is not to say that they are authentic. The historical question of which sections go back to Isaiah cannot be resolved by thinking about the quality of the different sections, but has to proceed by looking at the evidence the text gives us about its original context and date. There is room for plenty of honest agnosticism about such matters, and the fact that responsible scholars like Kaiser on the one hand and Hayes and Irvine on the other can differ so widely is a reminder that our evidence is much less substantial than we might wish.

Isaiah's Distinctive Message and Style

So far I have stressed the 'negative' aspect of the question of authenticity. Much of Isaiah 1–39 turns out on inspection to be rather unlikely to come from the prophet himself, because it reflects the concerns of a later age. It is equally important to emphasize that very few commentators (not even Kaiser) think that the authentic material is so slight that we attain to no real knowledge of Isaiah at all. Many of the sections that could be authentic, because they seem to reflect the situation in eighth-century Judah, also display a distinctive style and a coherent set of concerns which make it very likely that they go back to a single source; and if this source is not Isaiah, it is hard to know who it can be. As we shall see in the next three chapters, prominent among these concerns are:

1.   the political life of Jerusalem, and the policies of its kings and their governments, during various crises caused by the aggressive intentions of other middle eastern powers;

2. the ethical behaviour of people in Judah and Jerusalem—mainly but not exclusively the ruling classes;
3. what the future held for the nation, and whether this depended on possible changes in either ethical behaviour or political decisions.

There are important intractable disagreements among scholars about the third of these concerns, and especially about how far Isaiah predicted that God would one day shower untold blessings on the people—and if so, whether or not this would depend to any degree on their own response to him. But material in Isaiah 1–39 falling into the other two categories, 'political' and 'ethical' prophecy, is treated as authentic by nearly all writers on Isaiah 1–39.

With some passages there may be uncertainty about the exact date when Isaiah uttered them—hardly surprising at this distance from the prophet! But to take just one chapter, ch. 5: virtually everyone thinks that the 'Song of the Vineyard', a clever denunciation of the social injustices in Jerusalem (5.1-7), the 'woes' with their distinctive interpretation of the failings in Judaean society (5.8-25), and the prediction that the merciless Assyrian army will one day invade Judah (5.26-30), are a genuine record of Isaiah's own message. Isaiah emerges from the book as such a highly original and distinctive figure, that generations of critical readers have felt more than compensated for the 'loss' of the inauthentic sections—especially since they are not lost at all, but can be read as the work of later writers or prophets, who may also fully repay our study.

The Composition of Isaiah 1–39

Once we have decided, so far as possible, which parts of Isaiah 1–39 go back to the prophet himself and which are secondary, there still remains the task of working out how they all came to be combined, to make the book we now have. Here there is certainly disagreement, but most scholars adhere to one of only two models, and most probably see some truth in both of them.

Prophetic Schools

The first model (seen in the work of Jones and Eaton) ascribes great importance to the existence of disciples of the prophet. It is widely assumed that the great prophets must have had disciples; for as soon as we move away from thinking of the prophets as writers and see their original message as essentially oral, we need some explanation of how their words came to be remembered and recorded at all. Many scholars think that the complex transmission of the prophetic books, with layer upon layer of later material added to the original core of the prophets' own words, came about because each prophet's disciples came to form a kind of school. They made disciples themselves, and taught them the prophet's words together with their own additions to these. This process was repeated in each succeeding generation, until the prophetic book was stratified like an archaeological site. All the material claimed (not without reason) to go back ultimately to the named prophet, yet most of it was in reality the work of successive generations of his 'school'.

We know that in much later times the teachings of rabbis were transmitted like this. Teachers would utter sayings they themselves had composed 'in the name of' their own teacher or of *his* teacher, and would join these on to genuine sayings of some ancient authority, until discovering the actual date and authorship of any given saying became almost impossible.

It is not inconceivable that the prophetic books developed in this way. Isaiah may be a particularly good example, since it actually refers to 'disciples' of the prophet (8.16) to whom he entrusts a collection of his oracles to be treasured up until the time of their fulfilment, when his message will be vindicated. One of the most prominent proponents of a 'school' of Isaiah has been J. Vermeylen, whose major work on the subject attempts to trace the whole history of the school in minute detail. S. Mowinckel's traditio-historical approach also tended in this direction, though the circle of 'traditionists' was rather more widely conceived. The theory has the merit of accounting for the complex and composite character of the book of Isaiah, and of the prophetic books in general, while still explaining the fact that the whole collection was felt to be linked to the original named prophet.

The weakness in the idea of a prophetic school is its extremely hypothetical character. Apart from the one verse in Isaiah already mentioned (8.16), the prophets never refer to their 'disciples'. Furthermore, it is difficult to imagine what kind of social reality 'schools' of the disciples of the prophets could have had in Israel and Judah. How and where might their members have lived? Were they in effect 'prophets' themselves, or 'laymen'? Did they survive the Exile of the sixth century, and when did their work end? Satisfactory answers to these questions have been hard to find.

Scribal Editing

The alternative model thinks more in terms of the activities of *scribes* in Israel and Judah. Scribes had the task of copying any documents which had come to be of national importance. But on occasion they probably added to such documents as they saw fit. Once prophetic books existed even in a rudimentary form, they were at the mercy of the scribes who copied them, and may well have become a repository for ideas that had no specifically prophetic origin.

On this model we still need an explanation of how there came to be prophetic books in the first place, if the prophets themselves did not write. We know that Jeremiah had a secretary, Baruch (see Jer. 36.4), who seems to have been a scribe rather than a 'disciple' of the prophet. But should we argue: Jeremiah had a secretary, so perhaps all the prophets did? Or: Jeremiah *tells* us that he had a secretary, so it was probably unusual? It is impossible to be sure. But however prophetic books came to be compiled in the first place, once they existed their further expansion and editing may well have been a primarily scribal activity—the elaboration of a written text, not the collection of fresh (oral) prophecies. It was characteristic of ancient scribes to modify and add to the text they were copying, but not to rewrite it consistently in the way we might do in producing a second or third edition of a book, and this will account quite well for the often very complicated arrangement of the text in prophetic books. We need not posit generation after generation of disciples in a prophetic 'school'.

Such a gradual accumulation of material has been well described by McKane, writing on Jeremiah. He refers to a prophetic book as a 'rolling corpus'—like a snowball, which expands by picking up and incorporating new material into itself as it goes on its way. The 'scribal' model for understanding Isaiah 1–39 has been favoured especially by Ackroyd and Blenkinsopp. It makes most sense against the background of a more general theory about the editing, revision and interpretation of the Old Testament books. M. Fishbane provides such a theory, an account of 'inner-biblical interpretation', which shows that the prophetic books were subject to the same processes of redaction and reworking as the books of the Pentateuch, or the historical books.

Perhaps there are elements of truth in both ways of thinking about the composition of Isaiah 1–39. There do seem to be early small collections—for example, the so-called *Denkschrift* ('memorandum'—cf. Lescow) of chs. 6–9—which may have been put into their present form very early indeed, by close associates of Isaiah even if not by the prophet himself. At the same time, all the sections of the book include expansions which are probably 'scribal' in origin. These expansions originated during the redaction of Isaiah, just as is the case for secondary passages in other prophetic books—there is nothing distinctively 'Isaianic' about them. Some of them reflect the thinking of the exilic Deuteronomic 'school', which worked over many prophetic texts and was no closer to Isaiah than to any other prophet (see Perlitt). The Deuteronomists were certainly not 'disciples' of Isaiah, but it is from them that the narratives of 36–39 mostly derive, and their hand can probably be seen behind other insertions.

Some sections of the book may have originated not as expansions of existing words of Isaiah, but as the oracles of quite independent prophets: this may well be true of the anti-Babylonian oracles in 13–14. Such oracles must have had an independent transmission, probably quite unconnected with any school of Isaiah, until the day when a scribe decided to add them to the scroll of Isaiah. H.G.M. Williamson has suggested that the compiler of Isaiah

1–39 was in fact Deutero-Isaiah, the author of 40–55. If this is so, then material in 1–39 which resembles 40–55 must be seen not as scribal glosses to Isaiah, but as fully original prophecies by Deutero-Isaiah. They acquired their attribution to Isaiah when Deutero-Isaiah added them to the book, at the same time as he was attaching his own sixteen chapters of prophecy to it. To make the picture more complex still, we should remember that there are in any case similarities of theme between 1–39 and 40–55, and the (otherwise very rare) title of God, 'the Holy One of Israel', is common to both (and to 56–66). On the 'school' theory, Deutero-Isaiah might well be seen as a distant disciple of Isaiah, who knew Isaiah's oracles because they had been preserved in 'Isaian' circles for nearly two centuries.

A widely accepted hypothesis about Isaiah 1, first put forward by G. Fohrer, illustrates the complicated and fascinating course of the book's composition (see Willis for an alternative, but I believe weaker, explanation). Even a superficial reading of Isaiah 1–2 is likely to raise the question why the book seems to start twice, with rather similar 'titles' in 1.1 and 2.1. Fohrer suggested that ch. 2 was originally the beginning of an early edition of the book of Isaiah—not necessarily comprising the whole of 2–39 or even 2–12; and that ch. 1 was added subsequently. That is why it needed a fresh heading, since the original beginning of the book now became ch. 2. This clearly implies a scribal redaction of the book, operating at a literary, not an oral, level.

On the other hand, Fohrer did not think that the oracles in ch. 1 were themselves the invention of scribes. On the contrary, he thought most of them were authentic oracles of Isaiah. The editors had joined them together in their present order, and prefixed them to an existing 'book of Isaiah', but they had not made them up. They were to be seen as a carefully chosen *representative selection* of Isaiah's words, arranged not chronologically but thematically, and providing a short digest of the main themes of the rest of the book.

So, for example, 1.5-9 presupposes the 'Assyrian crisis' of 701 BC, with Jerusalem besieged in the midst of a devastated countryside, whereas 1.10-15 comes from a much earlier time, when Jerusalem still enjoyed considerable prosperity—

possibly before 730. The two oracles are linked by the catch-phrase 'Sodom and Gomorrah' (1.9-10), but they had quite different origins.

Just how deliberate the editing of the book was is a difficult question. Most commentators in the past have not seen quite so much design in many later chapters as Fohrer found in ch. 1. But in recent years (see Chapter 6, below) there has been a swing towards seeing 1–39 as a much more carefully structured whole, designed to convey a coherent message—and one which may have little to do with the intentions of the original words of Isaiah. Isaiah's prophecies have been made, by the way they have been ordered, into the vehicle of a quite different set of meanings.

Further Reading

On questions of date and authenticity in Isaiah 1–39 the 'maximal' view (virtually everything is by Isaiah) can be found in

*J.H. Hayes and S.A. Irvine, *Isaiah the Eighth-Century Prophet: His Times and his Preaching* (Nashville: Abingdon Press, 1987).

The 'minimal' view is represented by

O. Kaiser, *Isaiah 1–12* (London: SCM Press, 1972 [2nd, completely revised edn 1983]) and *Isaiah 13–39* (London: SCM Press, 1974 [second edn 1980].

In between are

*R.E. Clements, *Isaiah 1–39* (NCB; Grand Rapids: Eerdmans; London: Marshall, Morgan & Scott, 1980).
H. Wildberger, *Jesaja 1–12* (Neukirchen–Vluyn: Neukirchener Verlag, 1965–72), ET *Isaiah 1–12: A Commentary* (Minneapolis: Fortress Press, 1991); *Jesaja 13–27* (Neukirchen–Vluyn, 1974–78); and *Jesaja 28–39* (Neukirchen–Vluyn, 1978–82).

On the shape of Isaiah 1–39, see

*R.B.Y. Scott, 'The Book of Isaiah, 1–39', *IB*, V, pp. 149-381.
J.T. Willis, 'The First Pericope in the Book of Isaiah', *VT* 34 (1984), pp. 63-77.

On the identification of secondary material, see discussion in Scott and Kaiser, and the Further Reading suggested in Chapter 5 ('After Isaiah') below.

For the 'prophetic school' theory about the origin of Isaiah 1–39, see

D.R. Jones, 'The Traditio of the Oracles of Isaiah of Jerusalem', *ZAW* 67 (1955), pp. 226-46.

*J.H. Eaton, 'The Origin of the Book of Isaiah', *VT* 9 (1959), pp. 138-57.

S. Mowinckel, *Prophecy and Tradition* (Oslo) 1946.

For theories of scribal editing, see

*P.R. Ackroyd, 'Isaiah 1–12: Presentation of a Prophet', *Congress Volume, Göttingen 1977* (VTSup, 29; Leiden: E.J. Brill, 1978), pp. 16-48.

J. Blenkinsopp, 'Fragments of Ancient Exegesis in an Isaiah Poem (Jes. 2.6-22)', *ZAW* 93 (1981), pp. 51-62.

M. Fishbane, *Biblical Interpretation in Ancient Israel* (Oxford: Oxford University Press, 1985).

For further discussion of theories about composition, see

H.G.M. Williamson, *The Book Called Isaiah: Deutero-Isaiah's Role in Composition and Redaction* (Oxford: Oxford University Press, 1994); more fully discussed in Chapter 5 below.

Other works referred to in this chapter

J. Milgrom, 'Did Isaiah Prophesy during the Reign of Uzziah?', *VT* 14 (1964), pp. 164-82.

J. Vermeylen, *Du prophète Isaïe à l'apocalyptique* (2 vols.; Paris, 1977; a detailed working out of the 'prophetic school' hypothesis—see also the review by R.J. Coggins, *JSOT* 13 (1979), pp. 74-75.

T. Lescow, 'Jesajas Denkschrift aus der Zeit des syro-ephraimitischen Krieges', *ZAW* 85 (1973), pp. 315-31; on the origins of Isaiah 6–9.

L. Perlitt, 'Jesaja und die Deuteronomisten', in V. Fritz, K.F. Pohlmann and H.-C. Schmitt (eds.), *Prophet und Prophetenbuch: Festschrift für Otto Kaiser zum 65. Geburtstag* (BZAW 185; Berlin: de Gruyter, 1989), pp. 133-49; argues for a 'deuteronomistic' editing of all the prophetic books).

G. Fohrer, 'Jesaja 1 als Zusammenfassung der Verkündigung Jesajas', *ZAW* 74 (1962), pp. 251-68; Isaiah 1 as a summary of Isaiah's teaching.

W. McKane, *A Critical and Exegetical Commentary on Jeremiah*, I (ICC; Edinburgh: T. & T. Clark, 1986).

2

ISAIAH AND POLITICS

Prophets in the ancient world were frequently involved in the political life—and especially the foreign policy—of the nation. This is evident especially from the second-millennium Mesopotamian texts from Mari, where prophets advise kings in time of war and warn them of impending military disasters. There is also evidence of it in the pages of the Old Testament, where Samuel, Elijah and other prophetic figures are consulted by kings, or confront them unasked with a message of impending doom (see 1 Sam. 15.1-3; 1 Kgs 21.20-24; 22.5-28). The whole subject of political prophecy in Israel and in the ancient Near East is well discussed by N.K. Gottwald.

It is thus not surprising to find that Isaiah is recorded as having acted as an adviser to two kings of Judah, Ahaz and Hezekiah (see Isa. 7.3-17; 37.2-7, 21-35), and that his prophetic message contains much directly political advice. The same would be true, in the next century, of Jeremiah. Nevertheless Isaiah seems to have been so deeply involved in Judaean foreign policy that some scholars have suspected he was by profession a royal counsellor, who was 'called' from that sphere to a prophetic ministry much as Amos was called from farming or Hosea (probably) from being a priest.

Isaiah seems to have had ready access to the king (7.3, 10), and according to the narrative of chs. 36–39 the king sent to consult him when the Assyrians invaded. But the chief reason for thinking that he may have had a non-prophetic, official role at court is the similarity of his speech forms, and

of some of his ideas, to the 'wisdom tradition' exemplified in
the book of Proverbs. J. Fichtner and J.W. Whedbee argued
that Isaiah was a 'wise man' in the technical sense, someone
educated in the schools of ancient Israel, which are widely
thought to have trained civil servants to work in the chancel-
leries of the royal courts in Jerusalem and Samaria. When
Isaiah condemned the ruling classes of Jerusalem, and com-
mented on the country's foreign policy, he would thus have
been criticizing members of the social class he himself
belonged to. (Evidence of 'wisdom' thinking can also be found
in Isaiah's ethical assumptions, and will be discussed in the
next chapter.)

By no means all scholars see a connection between the
court and the wisdom schools (if indeed such schools existed),
or between the schools and Isaiah—see especially the discussion by R.N. Whybray. The case for seeing Isaiah as a royal
official is thus a precarious one. But the suggestion does
emphasize just how deeply the prophet was involved in the
political events of his time.

Isaiah lived in the period when the growing might of
Assyria, an eastern power occupying roughly the area of
modern Iraq, increasingly threatened the stability and independence of the small states of Syria-Palestine. In the ninth
century these states had been quite successful in containing
Assyrian expansionism, and in 853 BC had beaten off
Shalmaneser III at the battle of Qarqar; Ahab of Israel was
among the successful allies.

At that time, however, Assyria had become overextended
through the need to check the power of Urartu (biblical
Ararat) to its north. The decline of Urartu in the eighth century made it possible for the Assyrians to turn their attention to the west. 745 BC is usually regarded as the crucial
turning point, the year in which Tiglath-Pileser III took the
throne of Assyria and began a series of conquests which
would effectively wipe out Israelite and Judaean independence. It was because of Tiglath-Pileser's successes against
the Arameans of Damascus that Jeroboam II of Israel was
able to regain some lost Transjordanian territory (see Amos
6.13). Amos, it seems, was far-sighted enough to realize that
the weakness of Aram was good news for Israel only in the

short term, and in the long run created a power vacuum which the Assyrians would easily fill. Isaiah began to prophesy at a time when both the aggressive intentions and the military power of Assyria had become only too obvious. He counselled the various kings of Judah as they tried to handle the complexities of a situation from which, in the end, no good was likely to come to the peoples of Palestine.

It has become usual to identify four distinct periods in Isaiah's life when 'the Assyrian question' sharply disrupted life in Judah, and required a response from the spokesman of the national God. It is relatively easy to find oracles in Isaiah 1–39 that could well come from each of these four periods, though certainty of course is impossible.

The Syro-Ephraimite Crisis

The 'Syro-Ephraimite' crisis had its beginnings in the early conquests of Tiglath-Pileser, who captured Hamath in northern Syria as early as 738 (see *ANET*, pp. 282-83) and then quickly took tribute from the cities of Phoenicia and from Damascus, the immediate neighbour of the northern kingdom of Israel ('Ephraim') and the leading Aramaean (Syrian) state. Israel soon paid tribute in turn. Paying tribute was the least of the kinds of vassaldom enforced by the Assyrians, and involved no invasion or 'conquest' in the physical sense— it was not unlike paying protection money. By this means the Assyrians spread their influence and control by the threat of military invasion, without needing to expend forces on its reality. Paying tribute also had the effect of weakening the national economy, and consequently also the political institutions, leaving the country an easier prey if the Assyrian king later decided on a more aggressive policy.

At this stage Judah was not affected. However, in 734 Tiglath-Pileser moved west and terrorized the Philistine pentapolis. Judah was thus threatened to both north and west; Assyria, on the other hand, may have looked slightly overstretched. At all events in 733 Israel and the Arameans of Damascus decided to try to revive the old alliances of the ninth century and oppose the Assyrians through a 'Syro-Ephraimite' coalition. They failed to see how immensely

Assyrian power had increased, and how weak they themselves now were. Razon (biblical Rezin) of Damascus and Pekah ben (son of) Remaliah of Israel 'invited' Ahaz, who had just succeeded Jotham, to join the coalition. They intended if he refused to depose him, and place on the Judaean throne someone called 'ben Tabeel'—his personal name is unknown, as is everything else about him. As the northern armies prepared to march on Judah to implement this unwise plan (Hos. 5.8-9 may describe their route), Ahaz decided to send the Assyrians the tribute they had not (yet) asked for, to persuade them to intervene on his behalf. Whether on his behalf or not, the Assyrians certainly did crush the rebellion, which in any case they could not have afforded to ignore. Samaria was sacked in 733, Damascus in 732; Isa. 17.1-6 predicts both events. Judah was left free, but it had paid tribute, and this is not a reversible process: a request in the form 'Since you were evidently going to invade Samaria anyway, please may we have our tribute back' would not have met with a sympathetic hearing from Tiglath-Pileser. (The existence of a Syro-Ephraimite coalition has been questioned by R. Bickert, but the course of events sketched here is generally agreed.)

This period is the setting for Isaiah 7 and 8. The prophet's 'call', recorded in ch. 6, took place in the year of Uzziah's death, probably 741, but his first political oracles seem to have been provoked by the Syro-Ephraimite alliance, not long after the accession of Uzziah's grandson, Ahaz. (The chronology followed here is broadly that of S. Herrmann, based on K.T. Andersen, which is at variance with Clements, who follows Begrich-Jepsen. See the detailed discussion by J. Hughes). Isaiah goes to meet Ahaz 'at the end of the conduit of the upper pool on the highway to the Fuller's Field', perhaps implying that the king was inspecting the city's water supply in case of siege.

Isaiah's message to Ahaz has two aspects. The first is the symbolic *prediction* in his son's name, Shear-jashub ('a remnant will return') which will be discussed in Chapter 4. The other is the *advice* given to the king, which bears directly on the political decision he has to make. The advice appears clear: Do not fear, because God can deliver his

people; take no action to prevent defeat by the coalition (v. 4).
But there are two questions here:

1. What is the action Ahaz is contemplating, and which
Isaiah warns against? The king is told to 'take heed' and
'keep quiet'; what would constitute disobeying this advice? If
there is significance in Isaiah's meeting Ahaz at the water
system, it may be that the prophet was warning against
preparations for siege—put your trust in God, not in fortifi-
cations. Or he may have been thinking of preparations for
war—do not get ready to march out and meet the coalition,
but stay in the city and trust in God's deliverance. Either of
these suggestions could be interpreted as 'utopian', a word
which has often been used of the prophets, and of Isaiah in
particular, ever since its appropriateness was debated in the
1930s among German scholars. To ask a king not to defend
his city but to trust in supernatural intervention is indeed
'utopian', in the sense that no-one would expect it to be
heeded. It may still be what the prophet intended, for the call
to have 'faith' in God instead of in human devices is typical of
Isaiah.

But there is another possibility, and that is that Isaiah
was opposing not Ahaz's preparations for war, nor his plans
for fortifying the city, but his intention of sending tribute to
Tiglath-Pileser. If that is the case, then the advice could still
be based on opposition to trust in human power; but it need
not be utopian, since Isaiah could have calculated that the
Assyrians would intervene anyway. Isaiah could have been
saying that Ahaz had no *need* to do anything but 'keep quiet'.
A small indication that this may be what was meant is
Isaiah's advice not to *fear* Rezin and Pekah. If he were being
told to avoid military preparations, Ahaz could have replied
that he was not afraid of these two kings, but on the contrary
was taking appropriate measures to oppose them. But
sending to Assyria for help would indeed show fear, and it
may be this that Isaiah opposes.

2. But is Isaiah's oracle therefore an unconditional
promise, saying that the king has no need to fear, since God
will confirm him on his throne? Isa. 8.1-4 might tend to
support this: 'Before the child [the prophet's son, Maher-sha-
lal-hash-baz] knows how to cry "My father" or "My mother",

the wealth of Damascus and the spoil of Samaria will be carried away before the king of Assyria'. Or is it a conditional promise—which means, by implication, also a conditional threat? Isa. 7.4 and 7.7-9a suggest the former, but 7.9b, which seems intended as the climax of the oracle, gives a different impression. The sense is: Unless you *are* prepared to stand firm, you will not be confirmed or upheld in your position. In the Hebrew there is a wordplay on two forms of the root *'mn* (from which the word Amen is derived) and which is about firmness or constancy—the Jerusalem Bible renders 'If you will not stand by me, you will not stand at all'.

Thus the whole oracle is probably meant as a conditional promise of deliverance: *only* by not 'fearing', *only* by being 'quiet' (cf. Ps. 76.9), will Ahaz be showing faith in Yahweh, and thus deserve Yahweh's protection. Paradoxically, to be afraid, and therefore to seek help from Assyria, is the one certain way of not obtaining help from the one genuine source of help—the God of Israel. Political inaction is thus as much of an imperative, from Isaiah's point of view, as the political action which the king was pursuing seemed to him. (These matters are discussed further in Chapter 4 below.)

It is hard to know whether to say that events vindicated Isaiah or not. On the one hand, the Assyrians did save Judah, despite Ahaz's indifference to the prophet's word. On the other hand, Judah lost its independence and never fully regained it, which could be seen as a form of defeat. Isaiah himself seems to have regarded it in this light, as he also did later 'deliverances' of the nation.

The Fall of Samaria

The aftermath of the Syro-Ephraimite coalition was disastrous for the northern kingdom of Israel, which effectively became an Assyrian province, with only Samaria and its immediate environs left as a nominally independent but tribute-paying vassal state. Israel had long had a stronger tendency to insurrection and internal strife than its smaller southern neighbour, and in the years following the defeat of the coalition the monarchy there became highly unstable. This is the situation reflected in the book of Hosea (e.g. 6.11–7.7; 8.4). By 722 Samaria revolted from Assyrian rule, and the city was besieged, falling in 722 to Shalmaneser V. Judah was not implicated in this revolt, and so retained its status as a vassal, but with its own monarchy and administration.

Several of Isaiah's oracles may come from this period, notably 9.8-21 (+ 5.25-30, probably part of the same oracle, cf. Clements's commentary) and 28.1-4. Neither passage comments directly on the foreign policies of the time, but both evince much the same hostility to trust in human devices instead of in Yahweh that are present in the earlier oracles to Ahaz in chs. 7 and 8. The subjugated Ephraimites have lost none of their illusions of grandeur: 'The bricks have fallen, but we will build with dressed stones', they say (9.10). A similar self-satisfaction is condemned in 28.1-4. As we shall see, this is the kind of attitude Isaiah most typically condemns, wherever he encounters it.

Alliances with the Philistines and the Egyptians

The third phase of Isaiah's life saw Judah preoccupied with intrigues and alliances involving the Philistine cities and the Egyptians. From about 720, a couple of years after Samaria fell, Syria-Palestine experienced stirrings of rebellion against Assyrian domination. There were revolts in Hamath, the first state to fall to the Assyrians, and in Gaza, the farthest point of the Empire from their Mesopotamian power-base. The Egyptians saw advantage for themselves in getting involved, but nevertheless the king of Gaza was captured, and the revolt fizzled out.

But in 713–711 there was a further serious bid for freedom when the city of Ashdod tried to break the Assyrians' hold on the Philistine pentapolis. This time the Egyptians, under Shabaka, were deeply entangled; there were also negotiations with the more easterly Palestinian states, Edom and Moab, and Judah was certainly part of the alliance. This is widely agreed to be the background to the oracles in Isaiah 18 and 19. It is also the context for the story of Isaiah walking naked and barefoot through Jerusalem in ch. 20, dated to 'the year that the Tartan came to Ashdod', that is, 711—the year when the Assyrians under Sargon II finally stepped in to put the rebellion down. The events are briefly recorded in his annals—see *ANET*, p. 287. Ashdod was completely crushed, and the Egyptians time-servingly handed over the king of Ashdod, who had fled to them for asylum, to the Assyrians; but there is no record of any reprisals against Judah, Edom or Moab. If Isaiah's symbolic gesture, described in ch. 20, was meant to foretell captivity for his compatriots, he seems to have been mistaken, at least in the short term.

Most scholars think that Isaiah 18 has been worked over by a post-exilic editor; Kaiser indeed thinks that it is entirely post-exilic. But it is widely agreed that much goes back to Isaiah himself. It reflects the coming and going of ambassadors between Judah and Egypt in 713–11, and the vivid description of the Egyptians as 'tall and smooth' (v. 2) is likely to reflect the prophet's awareness that the dynasty to which Shabaka belonged was Sudanese in origin, though usually known now as the Ethiopian dynasty. The oracle is concerned with the pointlessness of all this frenzied diplomatic activity. In a memorable image we are shown Yahweh sitting quietly on his throne, observing it all, and biding his time until the crucial moment, like a great cat waiting to pounce—or, as Isaiah says, like a harvester waiting to harvest the vineyard at the precise moment when the grapes are ripe for picking. All that is seen of God is a gentle shimmering, like a cloud of dew on a very hot day, but the haze hides intense activity and preparedness to strike. Just as in ch. 7 we saw the needlessness and also the unwisdom of human political activity, so here we see its extreme folly. It is a silly but dangerous game which human rulers and their servants play, until the moment when God steps in to stop it dead.

Isa. 19.16-24 consists of five oracles about Yahweh's future purposes for Egypt, culminating in the extraordinary promise that one day 'Israel will be the third with Egypt and Assyria' (v. 24)—one of the most 'universalistic' oracles in the Old Testament, and perhaps also among the latest. Very few critical commentators think that any of this section goes back to Isaiah himself (see the discussion below in Chapter 5). But 19.1-15 could well reflect the same background as

ch. 18, Judaean negotiations with Egypt in 713–11. Once
again the pointless activities of the human participants in
political affairs are contrasted with God's capacity for pur-
poseful activity when needed, and his ability to turn all the
'wisdom' for which Egypt was proverbial into folly. Isaiah has
more to say about Egyptian 'folly' in the fourth crisis of his
life (see below), and this oracle could come from that time,
but its position between chs. 18 and 20, both reflecting the
third period, may preserve a genuine tradition that it is historically connected with them. Isaiah's political advice is
again that Judah should rely on God, not on human beings,
and he interprets this to mean that no alliances should
be made with Egypt. Isaiah's message in this crisis is thus
completely consistent with his attitude in the earlier days
when it was the alliance with Assyria that he condemned.

The Assyrian Crisis

The final phase in Isaiah's 'political' prophecy is also the
most complex and the most discussed. The accession of
Sennacherib to the Assyrian throne in 705 evidently seemed
to the Palestinian states to herald a weakening of Assyrian
power, or at least a time when determined vassals could
exploit possible tensions and uncertainties at the heart of the
empire. Along with the Philistine cities of Ekron and
Ashkelon, Hezekah withheld tribute, perhaps in consultation
with Babylon, then ruled by Marduk-apal-iddin II (biblical
Merodach-baladan), with whom he is said to have had diplomatic dealings (see Isa. 39 = 2 Kgs 20.12-19). Once again
Egypt was heavily involved, its promises of help as crucial
and as empty as ever. Thus Sennacherib was faced with
rebellion at the extreme western and eastern ends of his
empire. Since it took him four years to put down the
Babylonian rebellion and turn his attention to that in the
west, the allies had probably judged their moment well: if
there ever would be a moment for rebellion, this was it.
    Nevertheless in 701 Sennacherib was at last in a position
to invade Judah, and to involve the Judaeans in what is
usually called 'the Assyrian crisis'. It drew from Isaiah a
number of prophecies, broadly in line with his utterances in
the earlier periods.

The main sources for Isaiah's oracles are 28–31; 36–38, so far as the words there attributed to the prophet are genuine; and ch. 1, where vv. 2-9 are thought by many to come from this last period of Isaiah's prophecy. This oracle gives a graphic description of the state of Judah once Sennacherib's army had invaded, leaving Jerusalem the only unconquered city in a devastated country:

> Your country lies desolate,
>   your cities are burned with fire;
> in your very presence
>   aliens devour your land . . .
> And the daughter of Zion is left
>   like a booth in a vineyard,
> like a lodge in a cucumber field . . .
> If the Lord of hosts
>   had not left us a few survivors,
> we should have been like Sodom,
>   and become like Gomorrah (1.7-9).

Compare Sennacherib's own account of this campaign (*ANET*, p. 288):

> As to Hezekiah the Jew, he did not submit to my yoke. I laid siege to 46 of his strong cities, walled forts, and countless small villages in their vicinity, and conquered (them) by means of well-stamped (earth-) ramps, and battering-rams...Himself I made a prisoner in Jerusalem, his royal residence, like a bird in a cage [cf. Isa. 10.14].

Isa. 28.1-6, as we have seen, is probably an earlier oracle about the northern kingdom and its fall, and it concerns the social morality of the north (specifically its leaders' habitual drunkenness) rather than its political attitudes. But the chapter continues (vv. 7-13) with what seems to be an attack on Judah ('These also...'), reapplying the early, anti-Israel oracle to the southern kingdom during the Assyrian crisis. A similar use of the fall of northern Israel as a warning to Judah can be found in Micah 1, and in the lengthy reflection on the last years of the two kingdoms in 2 Kgs 17.7-41. Though the anti-Judah oracle also mentions the leaders' drunkenness, this is not so much condemned in itself as taken to be both a symptom and a cause of the political imbecility of the ruling classes. Isaiah sees the leadership as so befuddled that they believe they can defeat the superior power of Assyria.

The puzzling words of vv. 10 and 13 (RSV 'precept upon precept, precept upon precept, line upon line, line upon line, here a little, there a little') are probably to be interpreted as gibberish. The political leaders regard the prophet's message as nonsense, impossible to decipher. Or else the nonsense words may be some kind of mnemonic, possibly for the order of letters in the alphabet: *saw lasaw, qaw laqaw* could be part of a kind of 'alphabet rhyme', *s* and *q* being adjacent letters of the alphabet. The leaders' complaint in v. 9 is then that the prophet's message is childish, like a rhyme taught to children to help them learn their letters, not advice to be taken seriously by adult politicians. Isaiah's threat, in response, is that those who have refused to learn their alphabet from him in Hebrew will soon be taught it in a foreign language (Akkadian, or perhaps Aramaic, the Assyrian official language by this time): 'by men of strange lips and with an alien tongue the LORD will speak to this people' (v. 11).

What was this message which Isaiah's hearers had despised? It seems to have been much the same as in the 730s and the 720s:

This is rest;
        give rest to the weary;
and this is repose (v. 12).

Rest, quietness, stillness—the opposite of feverish political activity, which (to Isaiah's mind) served no purpose.

Isa. 28.14-22 has at its core the same political message: 'he who believes will not be in haste' (v. 16). It apparently condemns the alliance with Egypt as an attempt to make a 'covenant with death'—Death is a notoriously hard bargaining partner. The only true security comes from Yahweh, who provides a secure rock in Zion for those who trust him, but rejects those who prefer to seek safety in Egypt. In piled-up metaphors Isaiah paints a vivid picture of the horror that his audience will experience when the Assyrians come and sweep away all possibility of security: hail, rising floodwaters, a scourge, boots to trample them down, as they try in vain to rest on a bed too short to lie down on, under sheets too narrow to cover them. Seldom have mixed metaphors been so effective in conveying a climate of fear.

Oracles against the Egyptian alliance continue in Isaiah 30–31, again deriding the Egyptians and those who trust in them. Egypt is called 'Rahab who sits still'—the old ancient Near Eastern chaos-monster now turned to stone. The alliances of ten years before had shown how useless Egypt was as an ally, and it was stupid as well as faithless to seek help from Pharaoh. In another vivid compound metaphor the prophet compares the sin of Judah in relying on Egypt to a bulging wall, just about to collapse and smash into many useless pieces, just like a pot thrown down and broken so badly that no piece is left large enough even to scoop up water (vv. 12-14). The reason for this coming disaster is given in v. 15:

> For thus said the Lord God, the Holy One of Israel,
> 'In returning and rest you shall be saved;
>   in quietness and in trust shall be your strength'.
> And you would not, but you said,
> 'No! we will speed upon horses'...

A refusal to do nothing is again the primary sin of the Judaean leadership. 'Returning', *subah*, which later became a technical term for repentance, here seems to mean 'turning away from (military) activity', or perhaps 'turning to God'—see Clements, p. 248. Feverish activity, contrary to the divine demand for tranquillity, will find an appropriate punishment: the fast horses the people have purchased from Egypt will help them only to flee more swiftly from the battle they are bound to lose. Quiet confidence in God was called for; instead there was an insistence (arrogant, in Isaiah's eyes) on human wisdom, followed in the event by despair, and by the realization that there was no longer anything at all to rely on.

Isa. 31.1-4 repeats the same theme: 'Woe to those who go down to Egypt for help, and rely on horses'. Interestingly, the reason Isaiah gives for condemning the Egyptian alliance is not that it involves disloyalty to Yahweh. Other prophets did think along these lines—Hosea, for instance, may well have objected to foreign alliances as representing an attempt to gain help from foreign gods. But Isaiah's objection is that the alliance means trusting in *human* strength instead of in the power of God. Thus seeking the help of Egypt in 701 is wrong

for just the same reason as seeking help from Assyria in the
730s. It treats human strength as superior to divine
strength:

> The Egyptians are men, and not God;
>   and their horses are flesh, and not spirit (v. 3).

How far did the events of 701 vindicate Isaiah's words?
Two things are virtually certain. First, Jerusalem was not
actually captured by Sennacherib. The Assyrian troops went
away without sacking the city, and an oracle in Isa. 22.12-14
probably refers to the population's reaction: 'joy and
gladness, slaying oxen and killing sheep, eating flesh and
drinking wine'. But secondly, the context in which the city
was thus 'delivered' was such as to make these celebrations
'the unforgivable day of Jerusalem's complacency', as
Clements calls it. For many other cities had been sacked, and
Judah was never again to enjoy significant freedom, unless
perhaps for a time under Josiah, in the next century. If
Isaiah thought the city would be taken by storm, as some
oracles may suggest, he was proved wrong; but if he thought
that Judah would fail to win any fresh freedom, would be
deserted by Egypt, and would pay in many lives and much
wealth for its rebellion, he was proved right. Sennacherib
took a heavy tribute—300 talents of silver and 30 of gold,
according to 2 Kgs 18.14—which involved stripping gold from
the doors of the temple. Whether one calls what happened to
Judah and Jerusalem a deliverance or a defeat is largely a
matter of perspective. Isaiah, like the other prophets,
differed from his contemporaries as much in how he interpreted events as in what exactly he expected those events
to be.

But there is a much more difficult historical problem about
the Assyrian crisis. It arises from the puzzling inconsisten-
cies and duplications in the biblical narrative. The short
account of the events of 701 in 2 Kgs 18.13-18 does not
appear in the parallel account in Isaiah 36–37, except for the
introductory verse ('In the fourteenth year of King Hezekiah,
Sennacherib king of Assyria came up against all the fortified
cities of Judah and took them'). This account is broadly confirmed by Sennacherib's own annals (*ANET*, pp. 287-88). The
account which does appear, which is also in Kings, is a long

and rambling one. It culminates in a miraculous deliverance of Jerusalem and the death of the Assyrian army through the agency of the 'angel of Yahweh' (37.36). The Assyrian official, the Rabshakeh, makes two speeches in very similar words (36.4-20 and 37.10-13), Hezekiah twice consults Yahweh through Isaiah (37.1-4 and 37.14-20), and Isaiah twice prophesies the deliverance of the city (37.5-7 and 37.21-35). There are also strange chronological problems concerning the age of Tirhakah (perhaps too young in 701 to have been involved in the expedition mentioned in 37.9) and the date of Sennacherib's death, which is mentioned in 37.38 as though it followed immediately on the Assyrian withdrawal from Jerusalem, but which did not in fact occur until 681.

There was a time when the historical facts of the Assyrian crisis were regarded as a serious crux in Old Testament studies, with heated debate between the adherents of two main positions. One, which has now established itself among the majority of scholars, sees Isaiah 36–37 as composed of two parallel accounts, usually called B1 (= 36.1–37.9a + 37.37-38) and B2 (= 37.9b-36); the A account is 2 Kgs 18.13-18. B2 is then seen essentially as a heightened version of B1, in which the withdrawal of the Assyrians is explained not as the result of Hezekiah's paying tribute (as in A), nor even because they were urgently required for a war elsewhere (as in B1), but as a result of their physical destruction by Yahweh. Because B2 is much later than the events it purports to record, the presence of anachronisms is no cause for surprise. This explanation was set out in detail by B.S. Childs, and it has been refined and updated, within the framework of the 'Josianic Redaction' theory of Isaiah, by R.E. Clements.

The other theory was defended in detail by John Bright. It too recognizes that Isaiah 36–37 is not a single account of events in order. But it explains the duplications by arguing that there were two Assyrian crises, two invasions, two sieges of Jerusalem, and two deliverances. One crisis was that of 701, and it ended with the Assyrian's army's strategic withdrawal. The second occurred in the 680s, at the end of Isaiah's very long life; and it ended with the death of the Assyrian army through plague—referred to here as elsewhere in the Old Testament as the work of Yahweh's angel.

Bright's theory has sometimes seemed more attractive than Childs's to those with a more conservative approach to the Bible, since it does not entail that there are contradictions in the text, as the other theory does. Nevertheless it involves considerable amounts of imaginative reconstruction, and it produces an account of the historical events which is far from what the biblical text, taken as it stands, appears to imply. One advantage of it, as we shall see when we come to discuss Isaiah's predictions of the future, is that it makes it possible to see everything Isaiah foretold as having come true. The oracles attributed to him contain both promises of miraculous deliverance and threats of subservience to the Assyrians, and (with some ingenuity) it is possible to ascribe many of the latter to 701 and many of the former to Bright's second invasion.

But there is no Assyrian evidence at all to support the two-invasion theory, and not many scholars defend it nowadays. The general consensus is that B2 is a later version of B1, in which the story has grown in the telling. A tendency to invoke miraculous divine interventions is an observable feature of Jewish historiography, especially in post-exilic works such as Chronicles. The attempt to find a context within which Isaiah's oracles can all be declared 'right' should not lead us to multiply hypothetical invasions of Judah.

The events of Isaiah's life were complex, as the political allegiances of the state of Judah shifted and adapted to accommodate the realities of Assyrian power. His message, however, was remarkably simple and unchanging. It concentrated on a pure trust in Yahweh, which he believed must exclude all human attempts at self-defence and self-determination—whether these took the form of military preparations or appeals for help to one of the great powers.

Further Reading

On the political aspects of prophecy, see

*N.K. Gottwald, *All the Kingdoms of the Earth: Israelite Prophecy and International Relations in the Ancient Near East* (New York, 1964).

*J. Blenkinsopp, *A History of Prophecy in Israel: From the Settlement in the Land to the Hellenistic Period* (London: SPCK, 1984), pp. 38-79.

For Isaiah as a 'wise man' or royal counsellor, see

J.W. Whedbee, *Isaiah and Wisdom* (New York: Abingdon, 1971).

R.T. Anderson, 'Was Isaiah a Scribe?', *JBL* 79 (1960), pp. 57-58.

R.N. Whybray, *The Intellectual Tradition in Ancient Israel* (BZAW, 135; Berlin: de Gruyter, 1974).

On the historical background of Isaiah's work, see

*S. Herrmann, *A History of Israel in Old Testament Times* (London: SCM Press, 1975), pp. 227-62.

J.H. Hayes and J.M. Miller, *Israelite and Judean History* (London: SCM Press, 1977), pp. 415-34.

S. Irvine, *Isaiah, Ahaz, and the Syro-Ephraimitic Crisis* (SBLDS, 123; Atlanta: Scholars Press, 1990).

*R.E. Clements, *Isaiah and the Deliverance of Jerusalem: A Study of the Interpretation of Prophecy in the Old Testament* (JSOTSup, 13; Sheffield: JSOT Press, 1980).

B.S. Childs, *Isaiah and the Assyrian Crisis* (SBT, 2.3; London: SCM Press, 1967).

R.E. Clements, 'The Prophecies of Isaiah to Hezekiah concerning Sennacherib: 2 Kgs 19.21-34//Isa. 37.22-35', in *Prophetie und geschichtliche Wirklichkeit im alten Israel* (Festschrift Siegfried Herrmann; ed. R. Liwak and S. Wagner; Stuttgart, 1991), pp. 65-78.

*J. Bright, *A History of Israel* (London: SCM Press, 2nd edn, 1972).

On the chronology of Israelite and Judaean history, see

J. Hughes, *Secrets of the Times: Myth and History in Biblical Chronology* (JSOTSup, 66; Sheffield: JSOT Press, 1990), esp. pp. 159-232.

The effect of the Assyrian campaigns in the eighth century on Israel's neighbours is discussed in

J.R. Bartlett, 'The Moabites and Edomites', in *Peoples of Old Testament Times* (ed. D.J. Wiseman; Oxford: Clarendon Press, 1973), pp. 229-58.

Other works referred to or recommended

R. Bickert, 'König Ahas und der Prophet Jesaja: Ein Beitrag zum Problem des syrisch-ephraimitischen Krieges', *ZAW* 99 (1987), pp. 361-84; questions the existence of a Syro-Ephraimite coalition.

J. Fichtner, 'Jesaja unter den Weisen', *TLZ* 74 (1949), pp. 75-80, repr. in *Gottes Weisheit: Gesammelte Studien zum Alten Testament* (ed. K. Fricke; Stuttgart, 1965), pp. 18-26; the first to suggest that Isaiah was a 'wise man'.

H. Donner, *Israel unter den Völkern: Die Stellung der klassischen Propheten des 8. Jahrhunderts v. Chr. zur Aussenpolitik der Könige von Israel und Juda* (VTSup, 11; Leiden: Brill, 1964); classic study of political themes in the eighth-century prophets.

W. Dietrich, *Jesaja und die Politik* (BEvT, 74; Munich, 1976); Isaiah's involvement in political life.

3

ISAIAH AND SOCIAL MORALITY

One of the achievements of nineteenth-century biblical study
was to place the prophets' moral teaching back at the centre
of their concerns. Traditional Christian interpretation of the
prophets had stressed their inspired insight into the future
so heavily that the predominance of moral condemnation in
their teaching was in danger of being overlooked. German
biblical critics, especially J. Wellhausen and B. Duhm,
succeeded in showing that a concern for morality lay at the
heart of the prophetic message. The change of emphasis was
sometimes epitomized by saying that the prophets were not
(or were not just) *foretellers*, but *forthtellers*. They did not
(merely) predict the future; they linked their predictions to
an analysis, indeed a denunciation, of contemporary
society—declaring or announcing ('forthtelling') the faults of
the people they addressed.

The book of Isaiah is particularly rich in comments on the
moral state of society. These include both condemnations of
very specific actions, and also more 'high-level' criticisms of
the attitudes and predispositions that generate such actions.
As we shall see, there is an impressive coherence to Isaiah's
moral teaching, which brings what he has to say about the
ordering of society into harmony with his comments on
foreign policy (already examined in Chapter 2) and with his
attack on the cultic life of Judah and Jerusalem.

In Chapter 1 we saw that questions of 'authenticity' are
very complex in the case of Isaiah. But where ethical teaching is concerned, the problem is less grave. Most of the relevant oracles are assigned by almost all commentators to

Isaiah himself. There is not always agreement about their date. But many scholars tend to give an early date to oracles which are directed against the ruling classes of Jerusalem, especially if they imply a situation of national prosperity and self-satisfaction—likely enough before the Syro-Ephraimite crisis, but increasingly improbable from then on. If this is right, then most of Isaiah's attacks on the sin of his people predate his political prophecies, and belong closer to the years when Amos was conducting a remarkably similar polemic against the moral condition of the northern kingdom. After the early 730s Isaiah's attention shifted from the internal affairs of Judaean society to the political arena, and the nation's relationship with other countries—especially Assyria.

Sin in Isaiah

The best way to approach the ethical material in Isaiah 1–39 is to read through the relevant passages together, so as to get a synoptic picture of what the prophet had to say on this subject. The following passages form the core:

> 1.2-3, 10-17, 21-23, 29-30
> 2.6-22
> 3.1-12, 13-15
> 3.16–4.1
> 5.8-23
> 8.19
> 9.8-21
> 10.1-4
> 17.7-11
> 22.15-19
> 28.1-22
> 29.11-12, 15-16, 20-21
> 32.9-14

Naturally there is no complete unanimity among commentators about the meaning of these oracles, nor about exactly where each begins and ends. But it is not difficult to extract a list of the offences against God that Isaiah condemns, as follows:

1. oppressive treatment of widows and orphans—who may stand for all the weaker members of society (1.17, 21-23; 3.14);

2. theft (1.21);
3. murder (1.21);
4. perversion of the course of justice, by taking bribes (1.23; 3.9; 5.23; 10.1-2; 29.21);
5. expropriation of land belonging to the poor (5.8-10);
6. drunkenness (5.11-17, 22; 28.1-14);
7. excessive luxury and personal adornment, and the accumulation of wealth and status (3.16–4.1; 9.9-12; 22.15-19; 32.9-14).

This produces a 'profile' of the people Isaiah has in his sights (who seem to be mainly the ruling classes) which is similar to what we find in Amos. Those who have power abuse that power. On the one hand they oppress those with no power, who cannot retaliate; and on the other hand they exploit the opportunities for personal self-aggrandizement that power makes possible. This would certainly fit well into the relatively more prosperous times at the beginning of Isaiah's prophetic career, when the good days of Uzziah had not yet become a distant memory. But we cannot really be sure that the leaders of Judah abandoned their enjoyable lifestyle, even when the nation was being pressed from outside. Even in banana republics it is seldom the rulers who have to survive on bananas. At least one oracle, that against Shebna (22.15-19), could well come from the Assyrian crisis of 705–701. Some have speculated that Shebna was in effect Hezekiah's foreign minister, and that Isaiah's condemnation of him as an upstart with no right to a family tomb in Jerusalem ('What have you to do here and whom have you here, that you have hewn here a tomb for yourself?') was actually a thinly veiled objection to the foreign policy he had masterminded.

Already in this list, however, there are ideas which go further than those of Amos and rest on a slightly more developed vision of society. They seem to be less an instinctive and unreflective reaction to deeds that shocked the prophet, and more an analysis of social ills based on a coherent understanding of how society should be. For example, it is certainly true to say that Isaiah, like Amos, speaks on behalf of the poor and oppressed, and threatens their oppressors with divine judgment in the form of military conquest.

But the 'ideal' society against which contemporary reality is being measured is not an egalitarian one, as the modern reader of Isaiah is apt to assume. Nor is Isaiah a political radical, demanding a restructuring of the social order. The oracle against Shebna, just discussed, is a reminder of what has been called Isaiah's 'patrician' attitude. He was deeply opposed to social climbers with no long family tradition in Jerusalem.

In ch. 3 Isaiah presents his 'worst case' picture of Judah and Jerusalem, and it is not easy to tell whether he is describing the evils that currently afflict society or conjuring up a picture of the kind of society God might inflict on the nation as a punishment. (Often in the Old Testament divine punishment takes the form of confirming sinners in their sin—so this distinction is not an easy one to draw.) The worst Isaiah can imagine is a society in which ordered distinctions of status have broken down, in which 'the youth will be insolent to the elder, and the base fellow to the honourable' (v. 4), where 'children are their oppressors, and women rule over them' (v. 12). Indeed, this whole chapter and the next are marked by a concerted attack on the women of Jerusalem. It was apparently obvious to the prophet that no society governed by women could be a good society. Of course he may have had a particular woman or women in mind (the queen mother?); but the effect, to modern ears, sounds very far from radical. For Isaiah, it is a conservative society that knows how to protect the poor and helpless, probably through the principle of *noblesse oblige*. Aristocrats know how to treat people fairly; those new to power cannot be trusted.

Isaiah's condemnation of specific offences is thus set against a more general backcloth, in the form of a certain vision of how society should be. This society is one which perhaps had never existed in reality, in which people all knew their place and where the strong did not take advantage of their position in order to abuse the weak. Amos and Hosea idealized the period of Israel's wanderings in the desert, before the settlement (Hos. 9.10; Amos 5.25). But the fact that Isaiah's ideal society includes distinctions of rank makes it more likely that he is harking back to the kingdom of David, rather than to the 'Mosaic' period. It may be consistent with this that Isaiah seems never to refer to any historical events earlier than the time of David (see 28.21, possibly referring to 2 Sam. 5.17-25); and in Isa. 1.26, 'I will restore your judges as at the first, and your counsellors as at the beginning' is addressed to Jerusalem, not Israel, and presumably refers to the early days of the city under David.

Isaiah's Moral Vision: 'All Sin is Pride'

Isaiah's ethical denunciations are also broader in another way. In Isaiah, as in hardly any other prophet, we are told about the underlying *attitudes* or states of mind of those who are condemned. The 'woes' in 5.8-23 (+ 10.1-4) contain straightforward denunciations of social misconduct: 'woe to those who join house to house, who add field to field' (v. 8); 'woe to those who rise early in the morning, that they may run after strong drink' (v. 11). But also included are 'those who say, "Let him make haste, let him speed his work that we may see it"' (v. 19)—presumably this has in mind those who mock the prophet's warnings (cf. 28.9-10); 'those who call evil good and good evil, who put darkness for light and light for darkness' (v. 20); and 'those who are wise in their own eyes, and shrewd in their own sight' (v. 21). Mocking God, asserting one's own wisdom, feeling at liberty to reverse ordinary moral values, none of these is a specific offence in the way that getting drunk or taking bribes was. They are underlying attitudes or personality traits that predispose people to the specific sins which the prophet condemns.

Commentators have for a long time noticed that Isaiah offers a more integrated, less piecemeal approach to human sin than the other prophets, and have looked for some unifying theme. Perhaps the best suggestion for such a theme is *pride*. Walter Eichrodt wrote, '[for Isaiah,] the central sin of man lay in the overweening pride with which he set himself up against God...Luther's dictum *omne peccatum est superbia*, "all sin is pride", exactly sums up Isaiah's conviction' (*Der Heilige in Israel* [*Jes. 1–12*] [Stuttgart, 1960], p. 56, my translation). The essential sin of all the people Isaiah condemns is that they are *getting above themselves*. This applies equally to those who are trying to displace the

established authorities and take over the government (3.1-
15), those who prefer their own wisdom to Yahweh's (5.21),
those who seek to increase their own estates at the expense
of the poor (5.8), the women of Jerusalem who are interested
mainly in their own appearance (3.16–4.1—even if 3.18-23 is
inauthentic, its mock-heroic listing of baubles, bangles and
beads would surely have had Isaiah's full, maybe misogynis-
tic, approval), and Shebna, showing off his rock-hewn tomb
with a self-importance hateful to the prophet, to whom no-
one was paying any attention.

A basic concentration on pride also helps to explain otherwise puzzling passages such as 2.12-19, Isaiah's version of
the 'day of Yahweh', in which judgment is proclaimed against
'all that is lifted up and high' (v. 12, following the Greek
Bible against Hebrew 'low'). Everything that is 'high', including perfectly innocent trees, mountains, hills and towers, is
to be brought low. This surely makes sense most readily if we
take these natural eminences to be a metaphor for the
'haughtiness' of human beings, who are similarly to be
brought down (cf. v. 11) and abased. Indeed, the 'men' in
question are probably not human beings in general, but
Israel and/or Judah, whose leaders manifest just this quality
of overweening pride in their unethical conduct.

Pride or arrogance is also, in Isaiah's eyes, a mark of
stupidity or 'folly' ($n^ebal\hat{a}$), since people who are proud see
the world upside down, imagining themselves in the place of
God. Stupidity is pilloried in 5.21, as we have already seen:
those who are 'wise in their own eyes' are simply stupid in
God's. A similar condemnation occurs at the beginning of the
book, in 1.2-3: 'The ox knows its owner, and the ass its mas-
ter's crib; but Israel does not know, my people does not
understand'. The comparison of human beings with domestic
animals, to the advantage of the latter, has a long history,
and can be found in an Egyptian wisdom text, where the
pupil is told by the teacher:

> You do not hearken when I speak. Your heart is heavier than a
> great monument of a hundred cubits in height and ten in thick-
> ness, which is finished and ready to be loaded...The cow will be
> fetched this year and will plough on the return of the year: it
> begins to hearken to the herdsman; it can all but speak. Horses
> brought from the field have forgotten their dams; they are yoked

and go up and down on every manner of errand for His Majesty. They become like those that bore them, and they stand in the stable, whilst they do absolutely everything for fear of a beating. Even if I beat you with any kind of stick, you do not hearken (see R. Caminos, *Late-Egyptian Miscellanies* [London, 1954], p. 377; cf. also A.M. Blackman and T.E. Peet, 'Papyrus Lansing: A Translation with Notes', *JEA* 11 [1925], pp. 284-98).

Again, we are not told in Isa. 1.2-3 what specifically Israel has done wrong, but we are told that it adds up to 'folly'— culpable inattention to truth. As Robert Lowth put it in his great Isaiah commentary of 1778, these verses are 'an amplification of the gross insensibility of the disobedient Jews, by comparing them with the most heavy and stupid of all animals, yet not so insensible as they'.

Once we start to think in terms of pride or self-assertion as the essence of human sin, we may be able to draw together some other threads in the complex fabric of Isaiah's prophecy.

Sacrifice
Like other prophets, Isaiah has a certain amount to say about the sacrificial cult practised in Jerusalem. There is some evidence that Hezekiah undertook a systematic purification of activities in the Temple (see 2 Kgs 18.4), and if the speech of the Rabshakeh in Isa. 36.7 (= 2 Kgs 18.22) rests on any historical basis, Hezekiah may have attempted like his successor Josiah to centralize sacrificial worship in Jerusalem. However all this may be, Isaiah never mentions Hezekiah's religious policies, nor does he ever suggest that any of the cultic practices of his day are in the least acceptable to Yahweh; they are all condemned out of hand, just as they are by Amos, Hosea and Micah.

But what is *not* said is as interesting as what is said. In Hosea, Isaiah's contemporary, and in Jeremiah in the next century, the weight falls on the *apostasy* of taking part in a cult in which other gods are worshipped—Baal, Asherah or Mesopotamian deities. Isaiah also mentions this: see 1.29-30 (probably about 'fertility' religion), 2.6-22, 8.19 (on necromancy or divination by gods other than Yahweh), 17.7-8 and 31.6-7. Several of these passages are of doubtful authenticity. But all of them show a marked difference from the corresponding oracles in other prophetic books, in that they condemn the worship of foreign gods not as disloyalty to Yahweh but rather as the worship of 'what human hands have made'.

We have here the beginning of what was to become a stock tradition in Judaism, whereby foreign gods are identified with the images used in their worship and then described as 'idols', lumps of wood or stone, powerless to help their worshippers. The tradition begins in earnest with Deutero-Isaiah (e.g. Isa. 44.9-20), and develops in such texts as Baruch 6 (= the Epistle of Jeremiah) and Bel and the Dragon; but it is already present in germ in Isaiah. 'They worship the works of their hands, that which their own fingers have made'—it is no great step from this to the idol-maker of Isaiah 44, who cooks his dinner on one half of a piece of wood and then worships the 'god' he makes out of the other half.

All this is relevant to our present concern because it means that 'idolatry' or consulting other gods or other supernatural beings has been assimilated by Isaiah to the model of stupidity or folly, or indeed self-assertion and pride—for to worship what you have made yourself may look like extreme humility, but what is it really but worshipping your own face in a mirror?

Much of the worship in Jerusalem, however, was clearly not offered to other gods, but to Yahweh. Isaiah stands in the tradition of Amos in seeing even this genuinely Yahwistic worship as no more acceptable than the cult of other gods. And this is for the same reason. People who sacrifice to Yahweh are doing so to please themselves. (There is a good discussion of this theme by H.W. Hertzberg.) Amos had already said as much—'so you love to do' (4.5)—and Isaiah continues this tradition. Isa. 1.11 says that Yahweh has no desire for sacrifices (cf. Ps. 50.12-13); they are a burden to him, rather than a delight. They do not constitute a tribute paid to Yahweh by the people but are simply a means by which the people keep themselves happy.

This makes good sense within a general framework in which all sin is interpreted as somehow self-serving and self-ish—even though it looks rather implausible from a modern

point of view, since for us the very word 'sacrifice' has
acquired associations of depriving oneself of something. It is
worth remembering that sacrifices in ancient Israel were
'feasts' in a secular as well as a religious sense, and the
suggestion that people held sacrificial festivals because they
enjoyed them may not have seemed so hard to understand to
Isaiah's audience as it does to us. A sacrifice was not much
like Choral Evensong in St Paul's cathedral; sometimes it
was more like the office Christmas party.

Political Alliances
If Isaiah's condemnations of cultic worship, Yahwistic and
non-Yahwistic, make sense in the general context of his
attacks on pride and self-satisfaction, it is not a great step to
seeing his political message in the same light. One of the odd
things about his resolute advocacy of political neutrality and
non-engagement is that it is presented as the negation of
attempts at self-help. To us it looks as though Judah was
acknowledging its own weakness by appealing for help first
to Assyria and then to Egypt. Isaiah, on the other hand, talks
of this in terms of self-assertion. To him, it is a refusal to
trust in Yahweh, an insistence by the nation on pursuing its
own little schemes. The alliance with Egypt, condemned in
31.1-3, is wrong because it entails trusting human rather
than divine strength—'the Egyptians are men, and not
God'—and thus preferring the human to the divine, the crea-
ture to the Creator. This is essentially the same arrogance
that produces worship of idols or contempt for the rights of
others. Seen from this point of view, 'rest' and 'quiet' mean
not only political inaction and neutrality, but also an
acknowledgement of the majesty of God. What is required of
human beings, in effect, is that they allow God space in
which to act, and do not try to force his hand. Some more
theological implications of this will be considered in Chapter
6 below.

Oracles against Foreign Nations
So far we have considered only Isaiah's attacks on Judah and
Israel. But there are oracles, agreed by most commentators
to be genuine, in which he condemns other nations. Although

these are obviously not part of his 'social morality', they may
be considered here because they, too, fit well into the picture
that is emerging. Only two other nations appear in the
oracles generally judged authentic: Egypt (18–19) and
Assyria (10.5-19).

The Egyptians are condemned for folly (19.11-15), very
much as are the Judaeans with whom they were allied (see
Chapter 2 above). More interesting is the anti-Assyrian
oracle in Isaiah 10. Common sense might lead us to expect
an oracle against Judah's major enemy to condemn the
Assyrians for opposing Yahweh's chosen nation, on the principle that any enemy of Yahweh's people is necessarily an
enemy of Yahweh. In fact the oracle in Isaiah 10 is a good
deal more complicated than that. The Assyrians are not condemned for seeking to subjugate Judah. On the contrary,
that is said to have been a commission from Yahweh himself:

> Against a godless nation I send him,
>   and against the people of my wrath I command him,
> to take spoil and seize plunder,
>   and to tread them down like the mire of the streets.

The idea that Yahweh could use a foreign nation, the
Assyrians, against his own people used to be thought a
highly original one, and Isaiah was credited with the first
signs of the monotheistic faith according to which the one
God controls the actions of all nations, however great. But
the truth is more prosaic. It was not uncommon in the
ancient Near East for a nation's god to punish it by using
another nation. The classic case is the inscription on the
Moabite Stone (ninth century BC), where Chemosh of Moab is
said to have been angry with his land and so to have allowed
Israel to overrun it:

> As for Omri, king of Israel, he humbled Moab for many days, for
> Chemosh was angry at his land (*ANET*, p. 320).

The subtlety in Isaiah's oracle about the Assyrians is not
the fact that they were sent by Yahweh against Israel, but
that their commission had a fixed term, and that because
of overstepping it they now fall under condemnation
themselves:

But he does not so intend,
    and his mind does not so think;
but it is in his mind to destroy,
    and to cut off nations not a few.

Sennacherib is in due course to be laid low in his turn because he is saying to himself,

'By the strength of my hand I have done it,
    and by my wisdom, for I have understanding.'

By now we are moving into familiar Isaianic territory, and we are not surprised when the prophet breaks into rhetorical questions such as these:

Shall the axe vaunt itself over him who hews with it,
    or the saw magnify itself against him who wields it?

The Assyrians have not sinned by setting out to conquer Judah; that is just what Yahweh wanted them to do. But they have sinned by failing to see the divine hand behind their expedition, and by ascribing their successes to their own strength. In other words, they have sinned by thinking in much the same way as the rulers of Judah. Once again, therefore, the formula 'all sin is pride' seems to serve us well as a summary of Isaiah's moral critique, not only of Israel and Judah, but also of the Assyrians.

People sometimes object that it was absurd of Isaiah to think the Assyrians should have known they were but an instrument in Yahweh's hand. This objection is reasonable enough. But at least Isaiah does not say that the Assyrians had received a *revelation* from God telling them that they were only his instruments. He implies a more general idea, the idea that human beings are mere tools in the hands of God/the gods, which (at least in principle) many ancient Near Eastern rulers might have accepted, even if only with lip-service.

Divine Order

Thus there is a considerable coherence in Isaiah's message in both the political and the ethical sphere. Central to both is the idea that Yahweh, the God of Israel, is also the ruler of the world, and occupies by right the supreme position over all that he has made. The essence of morality is co-operation in maintaining the ordered structure that prevails, under God's guidance, in the world; and the keynote of the whole system is *order*. The task of individuals and of nations is to submit to their assigned place and avoid any challenge to God. H.H. Schmid has argued persuasively that the common prophetic terms *mišpāṭ and ṣᵉdāqâ* (usually rendered 'justice' and 'righteousness'—see for example Isa. 5.7) are the Hebrew equivalents of the terms many ancient Near Eastern cultures had for 'cosmic order', an idea which combined both religious and moral elements.

This idea is most familiar in the Egyptian form, *ma'at*, which is both the order inherent in the universe and a goddess. The king's task was to maintain *ma'at*, both by moral action—judging justly, maintaining the wellbeing of the country—and by diligence in offering sacrifice and organizing the ceremonies the gods required. When Isaiah speaks of the need for justice and righteousness, his words have undertones of this way of looking at the world, as a system whose order must be maintained by just and right conduct. Righteousness is thus a cosmic reality, not just an interpersonal one as it is for most modern people. Its neglect can be quite literally earth-shattering (cf. Isa. 24.4-5).

Sin takes its rise in disregard for this all-embracing order. The first and most obvious manifestation of this may be described as folly, ignorance, or perversity (cf. 29.15-16 *hopkᵉkem*, 'O your perversity!' or (RSV) 'You turn things upside down'). While the natural and animal worlds seem to observe due order by instinct, human beings ignore it. Folly produces a disregard for the orders in society which should mirror God's ordering of the created world. The result is anarchy, in which those with power no longer feel any respect for the claims and needs of others—especially those who themselves have no power, and no legal means to assert their claims. The practical effects are the crimes against social order which the prophet singles out: theft, murder, bribery and corruption, oppression of orphans and widows, enclosure of land.

Folly also produces pride and arrogance, which affects foreigners and Israelites, high and low. One of its cruder manifestations is the boastfulness that goes with too much drink; but it also engenders cynicism about moral values, and mockery of God. Pride makes people enjoy self-adornment and self-aggrandizement. In Hezekiah's minister, Shebna, it produces a quest for status-symbols; in the Assyrian king, a belief that he himself, not God, is the source of his victories.

In the political sphere folly leads to a false estimate of where true security lies for the threatened state of Judah. In the religious realm, it leads to the worship of 'idols', which is really the worship of oneself, and to a dependence on the sacrificial system, which in reality is equally self-centred, however apparently 'pious' in theory.

For Isaiah, a society which brings about its own downfall by its internal neglect of order and justice and its pursuit of self-interest, and then seeks to protect itself by inventing attractive and enjoyable religious rites, and by relying for aid on merely human powers, is simply walking in its sleep, and has lost its hold on reality. God can no longer get through to such a people, whose condition can best be summed up in two of Isaiah's most vivid images: the drunkard of 28.7-8, staggering in his own vomit, to whom the more plainly one speaks, the more one's warnings will be dismissed as childish babblings; and the Kafkaesque sealed book of 29.11-12, which the learned cannot read because it is sealed and the unlearned cannot read because they cannot read anyway. The intolerable sense of frustration that such perversity induces in the prophets reaches its climax in Jeremiah, who (it has been suggested) almost welcomed the exile of the sixth century because it was a return to reality, however harsh, after two long centuries of delirium; but we can already feel a similar frustration in Isaiah.

The Sources of Isaiah's Moral Teaching

How innovative was Isaiah's ethical message? In detail, Isaiah probably said nothing about the moral life of the nation that had not been said before. Three possible sources for his ideas can be readily identified:

The Tradition of Political Prophecy

Isaiah was not the first prophet in Israel, not even the first 'independent' prophet. Amos probably preceded him by twenty years or so, and Hosea and Micah were his contemporaries. There were certain issues that concerned all these prophets even though they may not have been part of any wider moral consensus in Israel. Most striking is the sense that the national God had a profound involvement in the politics, and especially the foreign policy, of his nation, such that to go against his wishes amounted to mortal sin for the nation's leaders. There was certainly a long prophetic tradition that spoke of divine involvement in political affairs—we see it already in the stories of Elijah, and in the account of Ahab consulting four hundred prophets in 1 Kings 22. Isaiah was not innovating in commenting from a religious perspective on the foreign affairs of the nation, and in seeing these as having a moral dimension. Even so, his message does have certain distinctive features, such as its emphasis on 'quietness', which we can gloss as political non-alignment in the name of total commitment to God, rather than to earthly powers.

Legal Traditions

The social teaching of the prophets, it is widely agreed, owes much to Israel's legal traditions, and Isaiah is no exception to this. Where nineteenth-century writers on the prophets tended to present them as almost the discoverers of morality, in more recent times it has come to be argued that many of the particular moral norms they refer to are already to be found in the various lawcodes of the Old Testament. They were not presenting the people with previously unknown moral injunctions, but calling them back to the morality they should have known well enough already.

The 'Book of the Covenant' (Exod. 21–23) may lie behind many of Isaiah's references to ethics. For example, Exod. 22.21-27 declares the responsibility of judges and rulers for the poor, the widows and the orphans—compare Isa. 1.16-17 and 10.1-4, while Exod. 23.6-8 condemns bribery and corruption, compare Isa. 1.23 and 5.23.

Furthermore, there are principles Isaiah seems to take for

granted which are not part of any existing lawcode, yet do seem to imply a legal or quasi-legal tradition. When he condemns those 'who join house to house, who add field to field' (5.8), he seems to be assuming that acquiring land from others is somehow wrong in itself—it is not said that this expropriation involves no payment, though of course actual theft *may* be meant. Probably Isaiah's attack on the rich has the same basis as in the story of Naboth and his vineyard in 1 Kings 21. There Ahab offers Naboth monetary compensation for his land—he is not intending simply to steal it—and yet Naboth rejects the offer, saying 'the LORD forbid that I should give you the inheritance of my fathers' (21.3). Ahab's eventual condemnation results from the fact that he (or Jezebel) actually gets Naboth executed on a trumped-up charge, so that all his property passes to the crown. But the hypothesis behind the story is that no one would be expected to part with ancestral property, even for the king. The inalienability of the family holding was evidently a principle with something like legal force.

The legal roots of prophetic morality have been thoroughly investigated, and good discussion can be found in the articles by A. Phillips and H.-J. Kraus. The prophets' dependence on law can be taken to imply that they were indebted to the theology of the covenant, of which the laws were seen as the terms and conditions. This is argued in R.E. Clements, *Prophecy and Covenant*. W. Eichrodt went further, and argued that Isaiah's use of certain metaphors for Yahweh—'father' and even 'Holy One'—show that he took the tradition of the covenant for granted. But in the last twenty years or so scholars have become less ready to draw such inferences. This is partly because of the arguments of L. Perlitt and others that covenant theology postdates the eighth-century prophets and partly because it has come to be seen that a use of the laws does not necessarily imply a use of the theoretical framework which certain Old Testament writers placed around them. We could think the Ten Commandments important without subscribing to the story of how they were revealed in Exodus 20. In the same way, prophets may have accepted and cited the laws of Exodus 21–23, without thinking of them as the terms of the covenant between

Yahweh and Israel. For a guide to the study of the covenant in biblical scholarship, see E.W. Nicholson's *God and his People*.

3. The Wisdom Tradition

Some scholars have suggested that the prophetic ethic owes a lot to the wisdom tradition. This would be specially likely in the case of Isaiah, if he was indeed trained in the 'wisdom schools' and/or employed as a royal counsellor. Isaiah sometimes uses forms of speech at home in the wisdom tradition, such as the proverb (e.g. 3.10-11—but this may be an addition) and the extended wisdom poem about trades or crafts (28.23-29, on which see Whedbee). But this aside, Isaiah certainly refers to moral norms that were more at home in wisdom than in the law.

One specific 'sin' condemned by Isaiah but nowhere mentioned in the law is drunkenness (5.11-12, 22; 28.1-8). It is a stock theme of wisdom writers: see Prov. 20.1, 21.17, 23.19-21 and 31.4-5. Attitudes such as pride and arrogance, which are so close to the heart of what Isaiah finds to condemn in his contemporaries, are in the nature of things hardly likely to occur in lawcodes—only a society with an Orwellian thought-police could legislate about such things. But the wisdom writers are primarily concerned with just such personality traits—see Prov. 21.4, 31.1-8, 13.10. Isaiah's condemnation of those who are 'wise in their own eyes' (5.21), sometimes read as an attack on 'the wise', is in fact a quotation from the wisdom teachers themselves—see Prov. 3.7.

What is more, many of Isaiah's moral norms that can be found in the law do also occur in wisdom. The obligation to care for the poor, for example, and the evil of condemning the innocent, are common wisdom themes, as is the condemnation of bribery. Even Isaiah's opposition to cultic sacrifice has parallels in wisdom: 'to do righteousness and justice is more acceptable to the LORD than sacrifice' (Prov. 21.3). The theory that Isaiah depended on wisdom for his moral insights is thus more powerful than an explanation in terms of the legal tradition, since it accounts for more of his teaching.

Despite this, it is probably safer to say merely that Isaiah was the heir of various traditions of moral teaching than to try to pin down one exclusive source for his ethical ideas. Anything taught in both law and wisdom could be described as 'in the air'—people could be expected to know about it without necessarily knowing *how* they knew it. This is how it is with moral traditions in our own society. People can seldom trace their moral convictions back to an identifiable source. Even when they think they can, they are not always right. Modern Christians, for example, often think that the moral values they hold dear are specific to the Christian tradition. But in many cases they can be found in many religious and non-religious cultures: admiring honesty, avoiding hatred of others, and caring for the poor and needy, to take just three examples, are common to many religions, ancient and modern, eastern and western, and also to many sorts of non-religious humanism.

Much the same may be said of Isaiah's values. Not only are they to be found in several branches of Israelite tradition, such as law and wisdom; they also occur in many texts from outside Israel. The obligation of rulers to safeguard the rights of those who cannot plead their own case (typically 'widows and orphans') is a commonplace of many ancient Near Eastern cultures—see the discussion in L. Epzstein.

When we have said that most of the details of Isaiah's moral vision can be found in earlier sources, we have not said that this vision is unoriginal. The synthesis outlined above, in which all ethical obligation derives from the divinely-given order in the world and begins with the acknowledgment of God as supreme, is not paralleled elsewhere in the Old Testament. Though there is no 'moral philosophy' properly so called in ancient Hebrew culture, Isaiah does emerge as a thinker with a strong drive towards a coherent and consistent understanding of ethics, well in advance of any other Israelite thinker known to us. The most distinctive feature of his system is probably the derivation of all obligation from the obligation to submit to God. This might well be explicable in terms of the prophet's own experience. Most commentators regard Isaiah 6 as an account of Isaiah's 'call' or prophetic commissioning, introducing the earliest record of his oracles, the *Denkschrift* (memoir) of chs. 6–8. This call takes the form of a vision of Yahweh in his heavenly court (cf. 1 Kgs 22.19), which the prophet experiences as an overwhelming aware-ness of the exaltedness of the holy God, and the sinfulness or 'uncleanness' of humanity in general, and of the people of Judah and Jerusalem in particular. Perhaps this contrast between the divine and human realms never left Isaiah, and constrained him to understand all sin as in essence the self-assertion of puny creatures against their exalted Creator. It would make good sense if this were so, though we can never know that it is.

Further Reading

On the study of the prophets since the nineteenth century, see

*J. Blenkinsopp, *A History of Prophecy in Israel: From the Settlement in the Land to the Hellenistic Period* (London: SPCK, 1984), pp. 26-38.

On ethics in the prophets, see

*C.J. Wright, *Living as the People of God: The Relevance of Old Testament Ethics* (Leicester: Inter-Varsity Press, 1983).
*J. Barton, 'Ethics in Isaiah of Jerusalem', *JTS* NS 32 (1981), pp. 1-18; some sentences from this are reused in this chapter.

On social justice in Israel and its environment, see

*L. Epzstein, *Social Justice in the Ancient Near East and the People of the Bible* (London: SCM Press, 1986).

On divine order, see

J. Barton, 'Natural Law and Poetic Justice in the Old Testament', *JTS* NS 30 (1979), pp. 1-14.

On the sources of Isaiah's ethics, see

A. Phillips, 'Prophecy and Law', in R. Coggins, A. Phillips and M. Knibb (eds.), *Israel's Prophetic Tradition: Essays in Honour of Peter R. Ackroyd* (Cambridge: Cambridge University Press, 1982), pp. 217-32.
*N.W. Porteous, 'The Basis of the Ethical Teaching of the Prophets', *Living the Mystery* (Oxford: Oxford University Press, 1967).
R.E. Clements, *Prophecy and Tradition* (Oxford: Basil Blackwell, 1975).
W. Eichrodt, 'Prophet and Covenant: Observations on the Exegesis of Isaiah', in J.I. Durham and J.R. Porter (eds.), *Proclamation and Presence* (London, 1970).

On the importance of the covenant for prophetic ethics, see

*R.E. Clements, *Prophecy and Covenant* (SBT, 1.43; London: SCM Press, 1965).

E.W. Nicholson, *God and his People* (Oxford: Clarendon Press, 1986).

German works referred to:

H.W. Hertzberg, 'Die prophetische Kritik am Kult', *TLZ* 75 (1950), pp. 219-26; on prophetic criticisms of cultic worship.

H.H. Schmid, *Gerechtigkeit als Weltordnung: Hintergrund und Geschichte des alttestamentlichen Gerechtigkeitsbegriffes* (Tübingen, 1968); classic study of the idea of a cosmic moral order in Israelite and other ancient Near Eastern thought.

H.-J. Kraus, 'Die prophetische Botschaft gegen das soziale Unrecht Israels', *EvTh* 7 (1955), pp. 295-307; important analysis of the prophetic condemnation of social injustice.

A. Alt, 'Der Anteil des Königtums an der sozialen Entwicklung in den Reichen Israel und Juda', *Kleine Schriften*, III (Munich, 1959), pp. 348-72; on landrights in pre-exilic times.

4

ISAIAH AND THE FUTURE

In everyday usage, a prophet is someone who predicts the future. Biblical critics have been right to argue that this is an inadequate way of understanding the great prophets of Israel. Isaiah, in particular, had an intense concern for the political life of the nation and for its moral life, and was certainly far from being merely a clairvoyant with supernatural insight into the future.

But it remains true that Isaiah, and all the prophets, believed that they knew better than their contemporaries what the future held. Prediction occupied a central place in their message. Modern biblical study has not really called into question the predictive aspect of prophecy in itself; it has concentrated attention on the *imminence* of the events the prophets predicted. It is obvious that Isaiah spoke of the future, in the sense that he told his hearers what they could expect to happen soon, what would be the immediate consequences of their present conduct; in that sense no-one would deny that he was concerned with the future. What is less certain—and what many biblical critics have questioned during the last century or so—is whether he also spoke of the more remote future, as is implied, for example, in regarding his book as a collection of 'messianic' prophecies. But scepticism about that should not lead to the extreme conclusion that Isaiah did not talk about the future at all.

No question in the study of Isaiah can escape the problem of authenticity. This is a familiar point by now. But where oracles about the future are concerned there are two special complications.

First, decisions about authenticity both affect, and are affected by, decisions about meaning. Thus one commentator may think that all predictions of the remote future are secondary, while another thinks them authentic. If they agree that (for example) Isa. 9.2-7 is about the future Messiah, then the first will think it secondary, the second genuine. So far, so good. But they may disagree about the meaning of the oracle. The first may think it is not messianic at all, but is about (say) the birth of Hezekiah (this is a traditional Jewish interpretation), and in that case may agree with the second that it is authentic, but for quite different reasons. (There are similar difficulties about identifying where oracles begin and end. For instance, does Isa. 29.1-8 consist of two inconsistent oracles, at least one of which is therefore likely to be inauthentic; or is it one unified oracle predicting defeat followed by victory for Jerusalem? Which alternative we prefer tends to depend on a prior perception of what Isaiah's message is likely to have been—and where do we get that from, if not from other decisions about just this kind of question?) There is so much danger of circularity in arguments like this that it is harder than usual to feel confidence in commentators' decisions, and we may suspect that there is simply not enough to go on.

Secondly, it is not as though Isaiah 1–39 contained oracles saying simply 'X will happen'. Some of Isaiah's predictions are presented as conditional on some action by his hearers, others are unconditional; some are of judgment, some of blessing; some foresee the possibility of averting disaster, others predict restoration after defeat—others again hope for the salvation of a 'remnant'. If we leave aside oracles where the historical context makes Isaianic authorship very unlikely (e.g. anti-Babylonian passages such as Isa. 13), we are still left with a range of predictions, and with few if any criteria by which to decide which were really uttered by Isaiah.

Five Types of Prediction

But if we want to know what Isaiah said about the future,
there is no alternative but to look for some way through this
maze. To make the task a little more manageable, we might
group Isaiah's oracles about the future under five broad
headings:

1. Oracles predicting certain defeat/disaster for Judah:
   2.6-21; 3.1-5; 3.6-8; 3.13-17; 3.24–4.1; 5.1-7; 5.8-30; 6.9-
   13; 7.17; 7.18-25; 8.5-8; 8.11-15; 8.21-22; 10.1-4; 10.22-
   23; 10.28-34; 18.1-6; 20.1-6; 22.1-8; 22.12-14; 28.1-22;
   29.1-4; 29.13-17; 30.1-17; 31.1-3
2. Oracles predicting certain deliverance (explicitly or by
   implication): 7.10-15(?); 8.1-4; 8.9-10; 9.8-12; 10.24-27a;
   17.1-6; 29.5-8; 30.29-33; 31.4-9; 37.6-7; 37.22-35.
3. Oracles predicting conditional deliverance: 1.10-17;
   1.18-20; 7.7-9; 30.15.
4. Oracles predicting restoration after destruction, or the
   purifying of the nation through disaster, or the restoration of a remnant rescued from general destruction:
   1.24-27; 4.2-4; 10.5-19; 10.20-21; 30.18; 30.19-26.
5. Oracles about the remote future: 2.2-4; 9.1; 9.2-7(?);
   11.1-9; 11.10; 11.11; 11.12-16.

(Category 4 sounds complicated, but it groups together all
oracles in which a coming destruction is regarded as certain
but restoration in some form will follow it.)

How can we move from these lists to gain some idea of
what the prophet Isaiah himself is likely to have said about
the future of Judah? There are two cautionary notes that
must be sounded at the outset. The first is that any reconstruction is almost bound to make the assumption that there
is something we can call 'the message of Isaiah'—in other
words, that Isaiah was a consistent thinker who had something distinctive and coherent to say, not someone who kept
contradicting himself. There is really no way we can know
this, just as there is no way of being certain that a single
word in Isaiah 1–39 goes back to the prophet. But to be
deterred from investigating his prophecies on grounds like
these would be a counsel of despair. We shall use a criterion

of consistency as one major tool in reconstructing the future
according to Isaiah, even though we cannot *prove* that it is
justified; almost all commentators do the same.

A second and perhaps more serious point is that we ought
not to assume that Isaiah said the same thing in each of the
political crises of his career. Indeed, the 'parable of the
farmer' (28.23-29) is sometimes interpreted as Isaiah's
justification for the fact that he did not. (J.W. Whedbee
makes a good case for this, while G. Fohrer thinks the parable is Isaiah's attempt to justify his own frequently changing
message to a sceptical audience.) Just as the farmer changes
tactics to fit the season and the crop, so Yahweh's plan
adapts itself to changing conditions. Hence, though Yahweh
is indeed consistent and wise ('wonderful in counsel and
excellent in wisdom'), he cannot be constrained by former
patterns of action. He must be expected to react freely to
events. There is, therefore, no reason why God (according to
Isaiah) should not have promised to save the nation from the
Syro-Ephraimite coalition, but then have threatened to hand
them over to Sennacherib thirty years later. Bright's solution
to the historical problem of the Assyrian crisis takes this to
its logical conclusion. There are, he argues, oracles predicting
defeat by Assyria, and others foreseeing deliverance from
them. But there is no contradiction, for the former belong to
the first Assyrian invasion of 701, the latter to the second
in 687. All that can be said is that *if* Bright is correct about
the two invasions, then both types of oracle could indeed be
credited to Isaiah. It would be less wise, however, to claim
that the existence of the two types in itself *supports* Bright's
theory.

A Consistent Message?

Each of the five types of prediction identified above must now
be examined, to see if any consistent message can be extr
acted, in spite of the difficulties just outlined.

1. Unconditional Doom
If we assume that Isaiah's message had at least a general
consistency throughout, then the first thing to observe from

the lists above is the great preponderance of unconditional predictions of disaster. It seems that, in each of the national crises he lived through, Isaiah foresaw defeat for the nation. It would be impossible to remove all the oracles foretelling 'woe' without reducing Isaiah 1-39 to a pile of rubble. Few commentators question that Isaiah prophesied ill for Judah—sometimes (as we saw in Chapter 2) with a severity that was not in fact borne out by events. Thus 29.1-4, assuming for the moment that it was originally separate from 29.5-8, seems to say that Jerusalem will be razed to the ground ('deep from the earth you shall speak, from low in the dust your words shall come'). Certainly nothing corresponding to this happened to Jerusalem at the hands of the Assyrians.

2. Unconditional Blessing
The much harder question is whether the unconditional promises are also authentic. Ever since the rise of modern biblical scholarship these have been under a cloud, because it is so easy to imagine reasons why later editors of the prophetic books would have wanted to invent them. By the New Testament period the assumption was widespread that the prophets had foreseen blessings for Israel. Ben Sira says 'May the bones of the twelve prophets revive from where they lie, for they comforted the people of Jacob and delivered them with confident hope' (Sir. 49.10). Of Isaiah he writes (48.24), 'by the spirit of might he saw the last things, and comforted those who mourned in Zion'—evidently referring to Isa. 61.2, naturally assumed to be by Isaiah, and treated as a good summary of the purpose behind Isaiah's prophecies. Any editor who saw the prophets' task in this light would be only too likely to ascribe oracles of hope and blessing to them.

Attitudes towards apparently unconditional oracles of hope illustrate well how difficult it is to be confident that our interpretation of the prophet is correct. The view that such oracles are mostly secondary has largely prevailed among critical scholars; but it has not solved the problem of authenticity, because scholars cannot agree which oracles are unconditional. All the apparently simple predictions of deliverance relating to the Assyrian crisis were treated by most older commentators as redactional additions, and are still so treated by, for example, H. Barth, for whom they belong to the 'Josianic redaction'. But G. Fohrer, who was equally sure that unconditional promises must be inauthentic, defended the view that *these* promises were not, in fact, unconditional—there were implied conditions. This is tantalizing for anyone hoping to discover that Isaiah really was a prophet of 'comfort': the hopeful oracles are rescued from those critics who would treat them as secondary, but the price is that they are no longer interpreted as very hopeful! (On this, see W. Dietrich's *Jesaja und die Politik*, and the review by Clements.)

It cannot be proved that the unconditional predictions of good things are all secondary, though what has just been said does suggest that it would be difficult to prove them genuine. Of those listed above, 10.24-27a and 30.29-33 would be widely regarded as quite late insertions—second-century according to Kaiser, though Clements argues that they cannot be later than the reign of Josiah if 'Assyrians' is taken literally. They exhibit some features of 'midrash'—exposition of scriptural passages by elaborating on them. In other words, they are probably later developments of Isaianic themes. Isa. 9.8-12 is implicitly an oracle of unconditional blessing for Judah, since it foretells the downfall of Syria and Ephraim—in other words, of the Syro-Ephraimite coalition; 17.1-6 carries the same implication. These two oracles fit well with Isaiah's message that Judah had nothing to fear from the coalition, and we will return to them.

Isa. 7.15 is dealt with below. Isa. 8.1-4 and 8.9-10 certainly imply absolute deliverance for Judah; but I shall suggest below that their juxtaposition with 8.5-8 should be taken seriously.

This leaves four unconditionally hopeful oracles, the ones on which most discussion has centred. All four seem to reflect the Assyrian crisis of 701, and three have the 'inviolability of Zion' as their theme (37.6-7 does not mention Zion):

> As when a hungry man dreams he is eating
> and awakes with his hunger not satisfied...
> so shall the multitude of all the nations be
> that fight against Mount Zion. (29.8)

The LORD of hosts will come down
   to fight upon Mount Zion and its hill.
Like birds hovering, so the LORD of hosts
   will protect Jerusalem. (31.4-5)

She despises you, she scorns you—
   the virgin daughter of Zion...
I will put my hook in your nose
   and my bit in your mouth,
and I will turn you back on the way
   by which you came. (37.22, 29)

This theme also occurs in the Psalms—see especially Psalms 46–48—and commentators used to regard this as clear evidence that the authors of these Psalms were familiar with Isaiah's teaching. Isaiah, it was believed, had prophesied that no harm would ever befall Zion, Yahweh's holy city; he was vindicated by events, when the Assyrian army was exterminated outside the city (Isa. 37.36-37); and Zion's inviolability to enemy attack duly became a received doctrine in Israel's theology, and found a place in the Psalms.

In more recent times it has become usual to argue instead that the tradition of Zion's inviolability preceded the days of Isaiah, and may even have been an old Jebusite belief about Jerusalem which passed into Judaean lore after the city's conquest by David. There are parallel beliefs in other ancient Near Eastern and classical traditions about the sanctity of capital cities. The Assyrian failure to take Jerusalem (whether caused spectacularly by a plague, or, more prosaically, by political events) was felt to bear out the tradition. It therefore continued to flourish until the sixth century, when the Exile killed it stone dead. In foretelling that the city would come to no harm, Isaiah was simply endorsing an already existing tradition, not innovating.

But neither of these possible ways of looking at the inviolability of Zion solves the problem of the authenticity of the oracles we are examining. There seems no reasonable doubt that Isaiah spoke *about* the inviolability of Zion, whether or not he depended on a long tradition of thought on the subject. But did he believe in it? One oracle that might be relevant here was discussed in Chapter 2 above: Isa. 22.12-14. This appears to comment on the popular reaction to the fact that Jerusalem did not fall in 701. Whereas people in general see this as a miraculous divine deliverance, and react by preparing great feasts of rejoicing, Yahweh is portrayed as saying that such a reaction is a mortal sin: ' "Surely this iniquity will not be forgiven you till you die", says the Lord GOD of hosts' (22.14). What the people interpreted as a victory, or at least a great deliverance, Isaiah regards as a disaster.

Both interpretations are understandable, from the different perspectives of the people involved. In straightforward physical terms, the difference between paying tribute to an enemy which then goes away, and seeing one's city sacked and looted, was immense—quite enough to explain why the inhabitants of Jerusalem were jubilant. They had lost the gold from the doors of the temple, but the city was intact, no-one had been killed or raped or tortured. From Isaiah's theological point of view, one outcome was scarcely better than the other; either way, Jerusalem was no longer independent, and the Assyrians would probably return before long. The point here is not to ask whose interpretation was 'right', but to note that this oracle suggests a prophet fairly cool towards theories of 'inviolability'. The city had not been violated, but for him it might as well have been. This may suggest that the Zion tradition, which continued until the Exile (cf. Lam. 2.15) received no encouragement from Isaiah. And if that is so, then it is hard to regard 29.5-8, 31.4-9 and 37.22-35 as authentic. They would seem to be either later additions, ascribing to Isaiah a belief in the security of Zion which he did not hold, or quotations from earlier 'Zion oracles' which are not from Isaiah at all—or at most are his quotations of promises he did not believe in and wanted to rebut.

In the last twenty years the pendulum has swung again. Clements, following Barth, thinks that the Zion tradition (which is in fact primarily part of the traditions about David and his dynasty) does not antedate Isaiah. It derives—just as on the older theory—from the 'deliverance' of Jerusalem in 701. It represents the conclusion that people drew from the non-capture of the city, and it was a disastrous one. The belief that the city never could fall to an enemy had very damaging results in the next century, encouraging the nation in pointless resistance to the Babylonians. Isaiah may or may not have said that Jerusalem would not in fact fall to the Assyrians; he certainly did not mean to say that it never could. Even if these oracles are genuine, they cannot bear the weight later generations laid upon them. Isaiah did not think that Yahweh had signed a blank cheque for Jerusalem, only that on this particular occasion he would bail her out.

This interpretation of Isaiah's unconditionally hopeful oracles leaves open the question whether they really go back to the prophet. But even if they do, they seem to be rather less dramatic and far-reaching than on a traditional reading of the book. Given the great number of doom-laden prophecies in the book, it is hard to imagine that in 701 Isaiah simply abandoned his lifelong gloom about Judah's prospects and became either the first exponent, or the willing representative, of the theory that Zion had an indefinite guarantee of prosperity and safety. And if he did give an assurance that the city would not fall—this time—then he was quick to insist that its escape was no victory, but the beginning of a decline into servitude.

3. Conditional Blessing

The conditional promises in Isaiah 1–39 are not numerous, but they may well be centrally important to an understanding of Isaiah's message. Isa. 7.7-9 is Isaiah's word to Ahaz during the Syro-Ephraimite war. Isa. 1.10-17 and 1.18-20 (if this is the right way to divide them) could be from almost any period, since they deal with social, not political matters; often they are ascribed to the period before the Syro-Ephraimite coalition. The first implicitly suggests that the nation may be pardoned if it reforms, the second says so explicitly: 'if you are willing and obedient, you shall eat the good of the land' (1.19). Isa. 30.15 clearly refers to the Assyrian crisis, since it stands in an oracle condemning the alliance with Egypt.

Isaiah's message during the Syro-Ephraimite war is hard to get in focus. We noted above that the oracles of Isaiah 8 (vv. 1-4 and 9-10) are promises with no conditions added. They speak of the certain downfall of the coalition. But on the other hand they now appear alongside 8.5-8, which is apparently an oracle of unconditional doom. It argues: since Judah has 'feared' Rezin and Pekah ben Remaliah, instead of trusting in Yahweh (symbolized by the gentle waters of Shiloah), the Assyrian invasion of the northern kingdom of Israel will spill over into Judah with a torrent like the waters of the Euphrates ('the River'). There is no particular reason to question the authenticity of either message, except for the obvious incompatibility between them.

It is just here that the *conditional* promise in 7.7-9 may provide a solution. Isaiah was in practice not simply predicting the course of events, but challenging the king and his advisers to adopt a particular course of action—or rather inaction. He presents a simple either/or. Trust in Yahweh will result in safety, appeal to the Assyrians in subjugation by them. The Syro-Ephraimite coalition will be annihilated by the Assyrians anyway—that is not the matter at issue; what hangs on Ahaz's decision is not whether the coalition will invade Judah, but whether the Assyrians will. We looked at the historical background to all this in Chapter 2. The core of what Isaiah has to say is the oracle in 7.7-9, which has a sting in the tail:

> It shall not stand,
>> and it shall not come to pass.
> For the head of Syria is [only] Damascus,
>> and the head of Damascus is [only] Rezin...
> And the head of Ephraim is [only] Samaria,
>> and the head of Samaria is [only] the son of
>> Remaliah.
> *If you will not believe,*
>> *surely you shall not be established.*

The enemy are nothing to be afraid of, but being afraid of them is! For that will lead to an appeal to Assyria, and that in turn will lead to a loss of national independence, and eventually to vassalage. Thus Isaiah's message is necessarily a *conditional* promise—which is the same as saying that it is a conditional threat.

The element of threat is most clearly seen in the presence at the conduit of the upper pool of Isaiah's son Shear-jashub (7.3). Both Isaiah's sons have ambiguous names. Maher-shalal-hash-baz (8.1, 3) means 'The spoil speeds, the prey hastens', in other words 'Military defeat is coming soon'. But

we are not told whether this is good news or bad. We are free
to take it as good news for Judah, because the hastening
army (of the Assyrians) will soon put paid to Syria and
Ephraim (8.4). But of course we could also take it as a
prophecy that this same Assyrian army will invade Judah,
and that is how it is interpreted in 8.5-8: it is Judah whose
end will come swiftly. Òne or other of these interpretations
could be a later addition, but if Isaiah's prediction was a
conditional one, we are free to regard both as authentic:
these were the options between which Ahaz had to choose.

So with Shear-jashub. The name means 'A remnant will
return', and the exact force of 'return' is not clear: return
from battle, return to Yahweh, remain in existence, these are
all possible renderings. The more fundamental ambiguity,
however, is how we are to stress the sentence. Does it mean
'A remnant *will* return'—'trouble may be coming, but all is
not lost'; or 'A *remnant* will return'—'only a handful of survivors will be left'? That either meaning is possible is shown
strikingly by 10.20-23, generally agreed to be a secondary
passage, where vv. 20-21 treat the existence of a remnant as
very good news—'A remnant will return, the remnant of
Jacob, to the mighty God'; while vv. 22-23 treat it as terrible
news—'though your people Israel be as the sand of the sea,
only a remnant of them will return'. As with Maher-shalal-
hash-baz, so with Shear-jashub, we may see the ambiguity as
deliberate. The king has the power to determine by his own
conduct whether the message shall be good or bad.

However, the ambiguity is not so complete with the name
Shear-jashub, because the very idea of a 'remnant' presupposes some kind of disaster (cf. Amos 5.3). There cannot be a
remnant of the people unless and until most of them have
perished, or at any rate become somehow irrelevant to God's
plans. Remnant oracles are potentially hopeful, after the
disaster has struck: they hint at new beginnings. But they
are not welcome in times when the general hope and expectation is that disaster can be avoided anyway. By taking his
ominously named son with him to meet Ahaz, Isaiah was
surely offering a warning: unless you heed my word, all that
remains of Judah will be rags and tatters; 'if you will not
believe, surely you will not be established'.

Isaiah thus seems to have offered the king a choice in the time of the Syro-Ephraimite coalition. Both his promises and his threats are contingent on the outcome of that choice. In principle the same is also true of the Assyrian crisis. Here again, Isaiah counselled non-alignment. 30.15 is the classic statement of his advice:

> In returning and rest you shall be saved;
>> in quietness and trust shall be your strength.

But the important thing to notice here is that this conditional promise now appears in the middle of an oracle which is not looking forward to a choice the king and the people still have to make, but back to an opportunity they failed to grasp:

> For thus said the Lord God, the Holy One of Israel,
>> 'In returning and rest you shall be saved;
>> in quietness and trust shall be your strength'.
> *And you would not*, but you said,
> 'No! We will speed upon horses',
>> therefore you shall speed away;
> and, 'we will ride upon swift steeds',
>> therefore your pursuers shall be swift.

Thus the promise of security through 'quietness' describes a course of action *already not taken*. Deliverance had been a theoretical possibility, but it depended on options the people had already rejected. Logically there is certainly a conditional promise in these words, but by the time Isaiah utters them he already knows that the conditions have not been met.

If we bear this in mind when turning to the two conditional promises in Isaiah 1, we may wonder whether even these are as hopeful as they look. Isa. 1.16-17 certainly exhorts the hearers to reform their ways, and logically must imply that there would be some point in their doing so: Yahweh would take note, and not impose the full weight of his punishment. Isa. 1.18-20 offers a straight choice between well-doing, leading to blessing ('you shall eat the good of the land'), and wrongdoing, leading to punishment ('you shall be devoured by the sword'—we might make the contrast more obvious by rendering 'the sword will eat you').

Some commentators think that the offer of forgiveness in

v. 18 is so out of keeping with Isaiah's message of doom that
we should see it as a rhetorical question—'Given that your
sins are as scarlet, shall they be as white as snow?'. Others
suggest that the prophet is quoting the people's claims in the
imaginary lawsuit implied by 'let us *reason*—that is, go to
court—together': ' "your sins are as scarlet, but they shall be
as white as snow"—is that what you are proposing?' But
these are rather desperate measures, for the verses do not
seem obscure. They seem genuinely to present a choice. What
we may wonder, in the light of 30.15, is how far Isaiah saw
the choice as still open. Was it perhaps one to which the
answer was by now a foregone conclusion, as with 30.15?
This might depend on when in Isaiah's career the words were
spoken. If they come from his early days, it is easier to imagine them as a real challenge than it is if they date from the
last period of his life, when he thought that Judah had
already had more than enough chances to repent, and had
thrown them all away.

Commentators' decisions on these issues depend in part on
(but also contribute in part to) their answer to the general
question, 'Did the prophets preach repentance?' Most readers
of the Bible probably take it for granted that the prophets
were sent to call Israel back to God, by trying to persuade the
people to change their ways. There is however a strong tradition of thought among some German Old Testament scholars
(see Schmidt and Hunter) in which it is emphasized that
prophets, in the eighth century at least, had the task of
explaining and justifying the coming judgment of God, rather
than of persuading people to act in ways that would avert it.
In this interpretation, even apparently straightforward
moral exhortations like 1.16-17 or 1.19-20 are not quite what
they seem, for they are really a statement of what the people
would have needed to do to avert disaster, but had, by the
time the prophet was speaking, already proved themselves
unwilling to do.

This goes against the common-sense assumption that a
prophet would hardly have bothered to prophesy if the
chance for repentance was already past. On the other hand it
accords well with another assumption, also common in
German scholarship, that the conviction of coming judgment,

rather than the moral analysis of society, was the primary datum in the message the prophets believed they had received from God. And it coheres with what is perhaps the most puzzling thing of all in Isaiah for the modern reader, the verses that follow the account of his 'call' in ch. 6:

> And he said, 'Go, and say to this people:
> 'Hear and hear, but do not understand;
> see and see, but do not perceive'.
> Make the heart of this people fat,
>   and their ears heavy,
>   and shut their eyes;
> lest they see with their eyes,
>   and hear with their ears,
> and understand with their hearts,
>   and turn and be healed. (6.9-10)

So far from Isaiah's mission being to persuade his hearers to repent, he is here told that it is to prevent them from repenting—to 'harden their hearts' and shut them up in their sins, so that divine forgiveness becomes impossible. This could be a retrospective interpretation, in which Isaiah looked back on his wholly unsuccessful attempts to induce a change of heart in both the moral and the political spheres, and reflected bitterly that the people's unresponsiveness must have been intended by God all along (see Clements)—or even that Yahweh must have deliberately set him up, rather as Jeremiah was to maintain a century or more later (cf. Jer. 20.7).

But Isaiah nowhere endorses our assumption that his mission was to be 'helpful', by talking the nation round to obedience to God. It may well be that we should take these verses very seriously as an indication that he thought his task was to point out the error of the people's ways, not so that they might change them, but so that they could have no excuse for what they had done, so that they could legitimately be punished by God, without being able to claim that he was treating them unjustly. This is a harsh and unappealing way of understanding Isaiah. But the prophets were strange figures, who often do not fit easily into the assumptions we bring to them.

Blessing beyond Disaster

To say that Isaiah foresaw no realistic possibility of averting disaster (or at best only a hypothetical one) does not of itself imply that he cannot have seen any hope *beyond* the disaster. In principle, oracles that look beyond defeat—a defeat which is presented as already certain—are quite compatible with oracles of unconditional doom. It is passages which expect the disaster to be *averted* which are the odd ones out. But 'hope beyond disaster' passages are not very numerous in fact. The interpretation already given of the name Shear-jashub suggests that 'remnant' for Isaiah was probably a negative concept—'a few left-overs'—rather than any sort of promise. In line with this, commentators usually treat Isa. 6.11-13 as foretelling virtually complete destruction of the nation: even if 'a tenth' remains in it, it will be no better than the useless stump left standing when a tree has been felled, and like such a stump, it will in due course be destroyed itself. It is a later editor who has added the gloss 'The holy seed is its stump' (v. 13), reinterpreting the useless survivors of the nation's destruction into the 'holy seed', the core of a revived nation. It was probably during or after the Exile that such a revision occurred.

A number of 'remnant' or 'restoration' oracles seem similarly to be secondary additions to Isaiah's oracles; among recent commentators, Kilian regards every single one as post-exilic. Isa. 10.20-21 has already been mentioned. Like 6.13c it seems to imply that the speaker is on the far side of disaster and can look forward to a new community centred on the 'remnant'. Isa. 4.2-4 is almost universally regarded as secondary (as are most oracles beginning 'In that day' in the prophets), and it too operates with the idea of 'the survivors', 'he who is left in Zion and remains in Jerusalem'. It is a rather midrashic passage, drawing on the imagery of the pillar of cloud and the pillar of fire from Exod. 13.21-22.

Perhaps the hardest of these oracles to treat as non-Isaianic is 1.24-27. This speaks of the coming judgment on Jerusalem as a *purging* or purifying, like the smelting of precious metal. It does not mitigate the force of the disaster that is expected, but unlike many oracles in Isaiah it does not see it as final. Defeat is the means which Yahweh uses on the way to implementing a positive purpose for Israel. The destruction of Jerusalem will be a step on the road to its eventual restoration, when Jerusalem will be 'as at the first', perhaps meaning 'in the time of David'. This is the first oracle we have discussed which envisages Yahweh's plan as having two stages (first destruction, then restoration), both intended and predicted from the beginning.

The same idea can be found in 10.5-19. Here the Assyrians are allowed to inflict suffering on Yahweh's people, but will then in their turn be punished for their arrogance, and Israel will reduce the Assyrians themselves to a 'remnant' (v. 12), plainly in the negative sense. Isa. 30.18, which is fragmentary, may express a similar expectation that Yahweh is waiting for the right time to restore his ruined people; and 30.19-26 imagines renewed mercy being shown those who survive in Jerusalem, though almost all commentators think it is from a later hand.

Two authentic oracles (1.24-27 and 10.5-19) do not amount to a very solid basis for speaking of a divine plan for the future in Isaiah's thinking, but such a possibility should not be ruled out. Though Isaiah's message seems mainly to have been gloom-laden, he was not committed in principle to uttering oracles of disaster, but to transmitting what he thought was Yahweh's word for the moment. There is no reason why he should not have looked beyond the disaster which he was certain would come, and foreseen a bright future for the survivors and their descendants.

Blessing in the Remote Future

There remains, finally, the handful of oracles within 'authentic' sections of Isaiah 1–39 which foretell blessings on the nation in a future remote from the prophet's own time. It is hard to find any way of connecting these oracles with the rest of Isaiah's message. If their authenticity is defended, this will mean that the prophet's teaching included both visions of great harmony and prosperity in the future, and a direct engagement with contemporary society, but made no connection between them. Why not? Alternatively, these oracles can be construed as not about the remote future at all. For example, the royal child to be 'born' (this perhaps refers to enthronement, seen as a new birth) in 9.2-7 may be interpreted as Hezekiah or some other actual king (see Clements, who argues that the introductory verse 9.1 also refers to very specific realities of the eighth century such as the partition of the northern kingdom by the Assyrians). Even the 'shoot from the stump of Jesse' in 11.1, which sounds as if it implies the prior demise of the Davidic dynasty, and hence must refer to an 'ideal' future king, *could* be thought of as referring to a contemporary royal child. Among recent writers both Wildberger and Barth adopt this interpretation, and so regard the oracle as authentically Isaianic. The wide consensus that such passages are secondary should not be accepted uncritically. But in general it is hard to see how they fit into any message we can plausibly connect with Isaiah.

The most famous 'messianic' oracle in Isaiah 1–39 is the 'Immanuel' prophecy of 7.10-17. In its historical context (the Syro-Ephraimite crisis) the oracle offers a 'sign' to Ahaz that Yahweh is to be trusted, not 'wearied' by the faithlessness of Judah's leaders; and this must mean that it originally had some contemporary reference. The birth of a child several centuries hence could not function as a sign of anything. But who then is the 'young woman' (construed in Mt. 1.23 as 'virgin') who will bear a child? Since the rise of historical scholarship two proposals have been Ahaz's wife—so that this is a prophecy of the birth of Hezekiah—or the prophet's own wife (cf. 8.3). There is no real evidence for either interpretation, and we could even consider the banal possibility that Isaiah meant 'that young woman over there', pointing to someone who happened to be passing. Also odd is the oracle's alternation between good tidings and bad. The fact that Ahaz has disobediently refused to ask for a sign would lead us to expect the sign given to portend disaster, but this is not so: 7.14-16 seems to foretell escape from the Syro-Ephraimite coalition. Yet 7.17 predicts an Assyrian invasion of Judah. The oracles that follow, in 7.18-25, are all predictions of destruction. But they are widely regarded as inauthentic.

The prophets' predictions of the future may be described as their *eschatology*, though some scholars reserve this term for the kind of 'historical plan' found in later apocalyptic works, where large stretches of history are seen as determined in advance by God. The term can quite reasonably be used in either way. If we use it to refer to 'that complex of teaching which arose from the prophets' conviction that Yahweh, the living God, was inaugurating a new action in history in relation to his people and to the consummation of his purpose' (E.W. Heaton, *The Hebrew Kingdoms*, p. 59), then Isaiah certainly had an eschatology. This is especially so if the oracles that speak of restoration beyond judgment are authentic, since then talk of a divine 'plan' makes obvious good sense.

But if by an eschatology we mean a detailed, many-staged plan for history, which does not necessarily have any connection with events in the present time of the prophet's speech, then it is probably anachronistic to apply it to Isaiah. B. Albrektson argued cogently that although Isaiah speaks often of Yahweh's plan in the sense of his *intention*, the thing he has decided to do, he never thinks in terms of a pre-arranged sequence of events which Yahweh is implementing, a 'blueprint' for action. Thus the 'purpose that is purposed concerning the whole earth' in 14.26—14.24-27 could be a detached piece of 10.13-19—is 'what Yahweh has decided to do about all the earth'. It does not (or does not necessarily) mean 'the comprehensive plan for the whole earth drawn up long ago by Yahweh'. It is arguably in Deutero-Isaiah that we meet this idea for the first time.

What cannot be doubted is that Isaiah 1–39 as it now stands does have an eschatology in the strong sense. This was produced by adding passages such as 11.1-9 and the other oracles just discussed, together with blocks such as 24–27. In its present form the book is as much an eschatological prophecy as any later apocalypse.

Further Reading

On the question of consistency in Isaiah's predictions, see

J.W. Whedbee, *Isaiah and Wisdom* (New York: Abingdon, 1971).

For the view that hopeful oracles are late additions, see

*R.E. Clements, *Isaiah 1–39* (NCB; Grand Rapids: Eerdmans; London: Marshall, Morgan & Scott, 1980).

On the question whether the prophets preached repentance see

A. Vanlier Hunter, *Seek the Lord! A Study of the Meaning and Function of the Exhortations in Amos, Hosea, Isaiah, Micah, and Zephaniah* (Baltimore: St Mary's Seminary & University, 1982).

On Yahweh's 'plan' in Isaiah, see

B. Albrektson, *History and the Gods: An Essay on the Idea of Historical Events as Divine Manifestations in the Ancient Near East and in Israel* (ConBOT, 1; Lund: Gleerup, 1967).
*E.W. Heaton, The Hebrew Kingdoms (Oxford: Oxford University Press, 1968).

Other works referred to:

H. Barth, *Die Jesaja-Worte in der Josiazeit* (WMANT, 48; Neukirchen–Vluyn: Neukirchener Verlag, 1977); a study of the seventh-century redaction of Isaiah's oracles in the time of Josiah; argues that hopeful predictions are generally secondary; mostly followed by Clements.

R. Kilian, *Jesaja* (Würzburg: Echter Verlag, 1986–); the most recent major commentary, still appearing; holds that most hopeful passages are secondary.

G. Fohrer, 'Wandlungen Jesajas', in *Festschrift für Wilhelm Eilers* (Wiesbaden: Harrassowitz, 1967), pp. 58-71; works with the hypothesis that Isaiah may have changed his mind about the fate of Judah from time to time, but that he had little hope for the nation's deliverance.

W. Dietrich, *Jesaja und die Politik* (BEvT, 74; Munich, 1976; surveys opinions on whether Isaiah's predictions were conditional or unconditional, optimistic or pessimistic; reviewed by R.E. Clements, *VT* 29 (1979), pp. 365-66.

W.H. Schmidt, *Zukunftsgewissheit und Gegenwartskritik: Grundzüge prophetischer Verkündigung* (Neukirchen–Vluyn: Neukirchener Verlag, 1973); argues that the prophets did not preach repentance.

5

AFTER ISAIAH

Scholarly fashion in recent years has moved away from such terms as 'secondary' and 'inauthentic' in referring to the material in a prophetic book believed not to go back to the prophet whose name the book bears. This is because of a widespread feeling that such terms tend to make readers think these sections less important, or less 'inspired', than the words of the prophet himself. In this book I have used these terms freely, as the most convenient way of indicating that some oracles are unlikely to go back to Isaiah. But there has been no intention of suggesting that passages 'secondary' in this historical sense are necessarily inferior in content. In this chapter we examine some of the sections of non-Isaianic origin in Isaiah 1–39, and also discuss in more detail than was appropriate in Chapter 1 the composition or redaction of the book.

Oracles against the Nations (Isaiah 13–23)

Several of the prophetic books contain a section in which a number of foreign nations are denounced, and their downfall predicted. This is already so in the earliest of the prophets, Amos (see 1.3–2.3), and the tradition continues in Jeremiah (46–51) and Ezekiel (24–32). Given the political concerns of Israelite prophecy from early times, this is not surprising. The prophetic word was evidently felt to be a powerful weapon in the hands of kings, and it may have been one of the essential functions of prophets to foretell—and thereby help to bring about—the downfall of their nation's enemies.

The story about Balaam in Numbers 22–24 presupposes that
a prophet could normally be employed by a king for this purpose: the whole point of the story is that Balaam is stepping
out of role when he refuses 'to curse whom Yahweh has not
cursed'.

But when we remember how many of the 'classical'
prophets of Israel spoke against their *own* nation rather than
its enemies, the occurrence in their books of 'oracles against
the nations' may on reflection seem rather surprising. In
Amos, they may be explained as part of a rhetorical tech-
nique. Amos declaims against the surrounding nations, as if
he were a normal prophet, purely (or at least primarily) to
lull the audience into a false sense of security, so that he can
then round on Israel itself in 2.6-12. But there is no obvious
parallel to this in the foreign nation oracles of later prophets.
They often seem intended to be taken 'straight', and have no
ironic intention. This, together with their sometimes rather
bland and standardized flavour, has long made commentators think that most of them are indeed 'secondary' to the
books in which they now stand.

Sometimes it could be thought that prophetic utterances
against foreign nations are drawn from a common 'pool' of
such oracles. Isaiah contains one lengthy oracle about the
Moabites (15–16) which is close to Jeremiah 48 (compare
especially Isa. 16.6-11 with Jer. 48.29-38)—just as Isa. 2.2-4
is more or less identical with Mic. 4.1-4. What is more,
although most of the nations mentioned were at some time or
other enemies of Israel, they were not all so at the same
time. The impression created is that these are rather stylized
collections of oracles. Each of them *may* have its origin in
some specific crisis involving Israel with the nation mentioned. But taken together they are more a declaration of
Yahweh's authority over all the earth than actual 'war
oracles'. And it is not impossible that some were artificial
from the beginning, written to complete a 'cycle' of foreign
nation oracles, at a time when Israel was not in a hostile
relationship with the nation in question at all.

But we need to be discriminating. Many scholars would
maintain that cycles of 'oracles against the nations' generally
began with an 'authentic' core, around which further

material came to be arranged with the passage of time. This is often said of Amos's oracles, where those against Tyre (1.9-10) and Edom (1.11-12) are widely thought to be additions to a collection that otherwise really is from the prophet's own lips. Much the same is said about the collection of foreign nation oracles in Isaiah, Isa. 13–23. We have already discussed a number of passages here against the background of Isaiah's own time—for example 17.1-6, which may refer to the Syro-Ephraimite coalition, and 22.12-14, usually thought to be a comment on the events of 701. The material in this section is so diverse in character that it is very hard to see it as part of a planned whole. This is not to say that it cannot be read coherently now, since the origins of a text do not necessarily constrain its later readers: on this, see Chapter 6 below.

Concerning Babylon (Isaiah 13 and 14)

One full-length study of these chapters maintains Isaianic authorship (Erlandsson), but most commentators think that prophecies of the imminent fall of Babylon presuppose the late exilic age (c. 540) at the earliest. This would make the author of these oracles a contemporary of Deutero-Isaiah. We can only obtain a date in Isaiah's lifetime by supposing that the Babylonians here are not yet the world-conquerors of the sixth century, but the vassals of Assyria who revolted against their overlord in the eighth (in 722–720 and 705–702). But ch. 13, especially if we link it with the next chapter, seems to be talking about the downfall of a mighty power, not the punishment of a rebellious vassal.

Isa. 13.9-16 seems to generalize the defeat of Babylon to produce a kind of world judgment on the 'day of Yahweh', in a manner otherwise encountered in 'apocalyptic' works, usually not before the third century BC (with 13.10 compare Joel 2.10). 'Babylon' soon became a cipher for any evil and oppressive power—perhaps initially through the prophecies of Deutero-Isaiah (Isa. 46–47), but certainly also through the present oracle. Thus, although anti-Babylonian passages cannot be earlier than the end of the Exile, they can easily be later. The book of Revelation, after all, is one long anti-'Babylonian' prophecy—only Babylon stands for Rome (see Rev. 17–18, and cf. 1 Pet. 5.13).

Isaiah 14 contains a lengthy 'taunt' on the fall of the king of Babylon (vv. 4b-20) which must rest on a mythological text about the fall of one of the gods from heaven: v. 12 is the origin of the Christian idea of the fall of the Devil (*lucifer* in Latin = 'day star'). The Babylonian king is described as modelling himself on one of the gods, and sharing in that god's sad fate. (Something similar is said about the king of Tyre in Ezek. 28.2b-19, again with use of mythological themes.) But before it we have two verses (14.1-2) that could easily be by Deutero-Isaiah, foretelling the restoration of Israel to its own land, the enslavement of the Israelites' captors, and (a new theme) foreign converts to Judaism. Isa. 14.24-27 may be Isaianic and is discussed above. The chapter ends with an oracle about the Philistines, conceivably from the third period of Isaiah's career (around 713–711), like the events of ch. 20.

Concerning Moab (Isaiah 15 and 16)

In 15.1–16.5 we encounter sentiments very unusual in foreign nation oracles, for the speaker is obviously sympathetic to the plight of the Moabites. Isa. 16.3-5 even seems to urge that fugitives from Moab should be given refuge in Judah and come under the protection of the Judaean king. This is thus not an oracle against a foreign nation but a lament for it. Only 16.6-7 gloats over the downfall of the Moabites; 16.8-11 resumes the lament, one of the most haunting in the Old Testament. Moab is treated as a (weaker) ally of Judah, not at all as an enemy.

Commentators have despaired of dating these poems. Extreme proposals have been that they are as late as the age of the Maccabees (B. Duhm) or as early as the reign of Jeroboam II (W. Rudolph)—i.e. before the time of Isaiah. Isa. 16.4-5 presumably implies that the Davidic dynasty has ended:

> When the oppressor is no more,
>   and destruction has ceased,
> and he who tramples under foot
>   has vanished from the land,
> then a throne will be established in steadfast love

and on it will sit in faithfulness
in the tent of David
one who judges and seeks justice
and is swift to do righteousness.

In that case it cannot be earlier than 587, and Rudolph must be mistaken. But the rest is largely guesswork.

Concerning Damascus (Isaiah 17)

The plausibly authentic oracle (17.1-6) has been supplemented, possibly as late as the Hellenistic age (after the fourth century BC) with fragments that condemn various forms of 'idolatry', including 'gardens for Adonis', part of a fertility cult (though see also 1.29-30, which may be Isaianic).

Concerning Egypt (Isaiah 18 and 19)

There is no reason to doubt that the core here consists of oracles from Isaiah himself, incensed by the alliances with Egypt that Hezekiah was embroiled in for over more than a decade, down to the Assyrian crisis of 701. 'Ethiopia' then stands for 'Egypt' as ruled by an Ethiopian (in fact Sudanese) king, unless (see Clements) the Ethiopians really were also in negotiation with Judah under the general umbrella of Egyptian–Palestinian plotting. But Isaiah 19 ends with five astonishing oracles which can surely not be by the prophet. Not only do they begin 'In that day', usually taken to be a mark of post-exilic, eschatological prophecy; they also reflect post-exilic relations between Israel and Egypt, where there was then a sizeable Jewish community. And the overall thrust of the oracles implies not defeat but salvation for Egypt, on a scale scarcely paralleled elsewhere in the prophets. It probably implies the existence of Egyptian proselytes connected with the Jewish temple at Elephantine, about which a certain amount is known from Aramaic texts found on the site (see A.E. Cowley, *Aramaic Papyri*). This would make the oracles probably of fourth-century date. The final vision of Egypt, Assyria and Israel as the three great world powers—and Israel listed third!—is unprecedented.

The narrative about Isaiah as a sign of the coming exile (Isa. 20) was discussed in Chapter 2; it falls outside the frame of the oracles against the nations.

Concerning the Wilderness of the Sea (Isaiah 21)

This chapter is famous for its words and cadences: 'Watchman, what of the night?'; 'Fallen, fallen is Babylon'; and most mysteriously, 'and a lion cried out' (v. 8—unfortunately 'lion' [*'aryeh*] is probably a corruption of the much less interesting 'watchman' [*ha-rôeh*]). But it is not famous for its message, which is highly obscure. There are detailed studies by R.B.Y. Scott and A. Macintosh. It could conceivably refer to the 'fall' of Babylon in Isaiah's own day (see above on Isa. 13–14), but it seems more likely that, as with other anti-Babylonian oracles, we are dealing with a prophecy from the late exilic age—again, contemporary with Deutero-Isaiah—cf. Isa. 46–47. Verses 1-10 seem to describe the emotional turmoil experienced by the prophet as he waits for the proclamation of the fall of Babylon.

The chapter concludes with three brief oracles about Arabia (the three districts of Dumah, Tema and Kedar). Perhaps they are linked with the Babylon oracle of vv. 1-10 because they come from a period when Judah and Arabia were alike suffering under the Babylonians—again, the late sixth century is possible. But such tiny fragments tell us very little.

Concerning the Valley of Vision (Isaiah 22)

Here again there is probably an Isaianic core, connected with the Assyrian crisis, as discussed in Chapter 2; but there are several additions. The prose insertion, vv. 8b-11, is particularly interesting. It could be referring to precautions taken in the time of the Syro-Ephraimite coalition, so that we might connect it with Ahaz's inspection of the water supply, possibly implied in Isa. 7.4. But Clements rightly comments, 'These verses presuppose the downfall of Jerusalem, not its deliverance' (p. 182). They are hardly an independent oracle, more an editorial addition drawing a conscious parallel between the escape of Jerusalem in 701, which had led to a belief in its inviolability, and Yahweh's failure to defend it in 587. In good Isaianic manner, it traces this latter failure to the people's neglect of Yahweh and his plans or intentions, preferring their own cleverness, and trusting in their own power to fortify the city. This editor was not Isaiah, but he had understood him.

Concerning Tyre (Isaiah 23)

Oracles against Tyre also occur in Ezekiel (26–28). Tyre was besieged by Nebuchadnezzar from 585–573, so that Ezekiel was a contemporary observer of the sufferings of Tyre, which however did not fall (see Ezek. 29.17-20). It seems that Isa. 23.13 must belong to this period, reinterpreting the Tyre oracle that precedes it (vv. 1-12) by stating that this really referred to Tyre's conquest by Babylon, not by Assyria. (Presumably the verse comes from the actual years of the siege of Tyre, since it assumes this will be successful, which was not the case.) But this logically implies that the original oracle is earlier than the 580s, and reflects a previous siege in which the enemy really was Assyria. Sennacherib attacked Phoenicia in 705–701 as part of the same series of campaigns that brought him to the gates of Jerusalem; and Esarhaddon destroyed Sidon in 678. So vv. 1-12 could be pre-exilic, and could even be by Isaiah, though the oracle bears little resemblance to any other authentic oracles. Verses 14-18 are later embellishments.

Two obvious tendencies in chs. 13–23 are (a) the systematic grouping of oracles by subject matter but without regard to chronology, and (b) a desire to gloss, comment and update. The effect is to generate a strong sense of unity in material which is actually quite disparate, but at the cost of seeing everything in a soft, even blurred focus. The result is a text which is well equipped to answer questions such as 'What is the word of the Lord about proud and rebellious nations?' but very unhelpful if we want to know what Isaiah said on any particular occasion about a certain battle, and whether he was right. Critical scholarship, like critical history of all kinds, sets out to discover precisely those things the authors did not want us to know; and considering the character of the biblical text, it has achieved a remarkable measure of success. But when we examine the redaction history of a book like Isaiah, we soon realize why it is so much easier to ask about the general theological message. It is easier because that is what the editors wanted us to do. They corrected the text, reduced its specificity, and generalized it to the point where we can no longer at all readily ask whether or not its predictions or warnings were 'correct'.

The Isaiah Apocalypse (Isaiah 24–27)

It has long been customary to describe Isaiah 24–27 as 'the Isaiah (or Isaian) Apocalypse'. The grounds are simple. These chapters contain a view of the future which has a universal, not just national or even international, scope (e.g. 24.21, 25.7-8); and they envisage manifestations of God's power in the cosmic as well as the political sphere—'for the windows of heaven are opened, and the foundations of the earth tremble' (24.18b). Both of these are features we associate with so-called 'apocalyptic' literature like Daniel, Enoch and the book of Revelation. The chapters have enough features of common style, and are sufficiently marked off from the oracles preceding and following, for commentators to see them as a coherent unit. But the alternation of prose and verse, and the lack of any logical structure of thought, means that few would now share Lindblom's belief that this is a deliberate, free composition. Fohrer too takes this line, and also agrees with Lindblom in seeing the work as a liturgical composition (Lindblom called it a 'cantata'). Recent commentators (Kaiser, Wildberger, Vermeylen) see it as more fragmented, and are sceptical about the proposed liturgical origin.

As usual, there is a wide diversity of theories about the origins of this apocalypse. But, interestingly, the disagreement is not just about the date and context of its composition. On this opinions do indeed diverge very widely, with Kaiser following in Duhm's steps and postulating a Maccabean date (so that the collection is roughly contemporary with Daniel), while others have dated it to the end of the Exile, taking the city which falls in 25.1-5 as Babylon—thus giving us another section of Isaiah 1–39 from the time of Deutero-Isaiah. But there is also a difference of scholarly opinion on whether the work formed an already finished whole which was then added to the embryonic book of Isaiah, or whether some at least of it was composed with its present location in mind.

Most commentators think that a small original core did have an independent existence. Wildberger identifies this *Grundwerk*, basic document, as consisting of 24.1-6, 24.14-20 and 26.7-21. These passages are a product of the early post-exilic period, when the newly refounded 'Israel'—Jerusalem and parts of the old territory of Judah—was under the authority of the Persians. This document enshrined a vision of God's judgment on the world and eventual conquest of the power of suffering and death, but it never had any specific city or nation in view, nor was it a prophecy of some imminent event. Like other 'proto-apocalyptic' works (Joel, Zech. 9–14) it showed a studied vagueness about times and places, and was concerned more with a general assurance that God's kingdom would one day be inaugurated on earth and in heaven.

But the extensive additions which have produced the present four chapters may well be part of the work's incorporation into the book of Isaiah. This would explain why there are often allusions to themes from the prophecy of Isaiah. The most striking is in 27.2-5, where the 'Song of the Vineyard' (5.1-7) is reversed: whereas in the eighth century Isaiah had portrayed Judah as an unrewarding vineyard yielding nothing but 'wild grapes', now the vineyard which is the new Israel is so pleasant that Yahweh actually wishes he had difficulties to overcome! Israel has become once again God's prize possession. But some commentators (e.g. Clements) not only maintain that the Isaiah Apocalypse is in essence a deliberate addition to Isaiah, but also argue that it is specifically designed for its present position in the book, following the oracles on the nations of chs. 13–23. The editors who added the apocalypse believed that the crucial moment in world history was about to dawn, when Israel's fortunes would at last be reversed and all opposing powers frustrated. The 'oracles' they added in 24–27 were always meant to be read alongside the earlier (supposedly all Isaianic) prophecies in 1–23.

This is an important idea from the modern hermeneutical perspective, not just from the standpoint of historical exegesis. Earlier commentators took it for granted that the Isaiah Apocalypse was originally a self-contained work—Lindblom's 'cantata' theory, for example, makes no sense on any other hypothesis. The trend in Isaiah studies at present is in the opposite direction. Scholars tend now not to believe that the non-Isaianic material in the book was (for the most part) the

work of older 'authors', in principle just as independent as
Isaiah himself. Instead they often believe that such material
comes from the pens of the same people as does the final or
semi-final edition of the book of Isaiah. Many of the redactors
of Isaiah, on this view, were not adding *existing* works to
the words of Isaiah. They were writing additional sections
themselves—though admittedly these sections did sometimes
have a core which the redactors had not themselves
invented, as is the case in 24–27. In Pentateuchal studies we
distinguish carefully between 'source' theories, where the
redactor wove together already existing material with
slight modifications, and 'supplementary' theories, which
see redactors as more creative figures, writing their own
additional material as required. But in the study of the
prophets the difference is sometimes not perceived quite so
clearly, though it would be helpful if it were. The trend,
anyway, is now towards 'supplementary' theories of the
development of the prophetic books, and current discussion
of the Isaiah Apocalypse is a good example of this.

If chs. 24–27 have an early post-exilic core, but in their
present form belong to a redaction later than that which
added 13–23 to 1–12, then they probably come from well on
in the Persian period—the late fifth or early fourth century.
The Isaiah Apocalypse shows many of the characteristic
beliefs of Jewish eschatological thinking. These include
Yahweh's coming dominion over all the world, the downfall of
all hostile powers, the helplessness of the Jewish community
who can only wait for God to act, Yahweh's power even over
the realm of the dead (cf. 25.8, 26.19—though these may be
still later additions), the participation of the whole cosmos
in the final divine drama, and the gathering in of all the
dispersed of Israel—the vision with which the section ends:

> And in that day a great trumpet will be blown, and those who
> were lost in the land of Assyria and those who were driven out to
> the land of Egypt will come and worship the Lord on the holy
> mountain at Jerusalem. (27.13)

The 'Little Apocalypse' (Isaiah 34–35)

The third major block of non-Isaianic oracles in 1–39 consists
of chs. 34 and 35. Isaiah 34 is a macabre prophecy of

judgment on Edom (vv. 5-17), reminiscent in some ways of the anti-Babylonian oracle in Isaiah 13 (compare 34.11 with 13.21-22). But it is introduced with what, out of context, would naturally be interpreted as an 'apocalyptic' prediction (vv. 1-4), in which all the nations are judged (v. 2) and the heavens themselves 'shall rot away, and the skies roll up like a scroll' (v. 4a). Hence the name 'Little Apocalypse'—little because shorter than 24–27, but just as apocalyptic. The 'universal' and 'Edomite' sections of the chapter are not to be seen as originally separate: judgment on Edom is the 'cash value' of the predicted cosmic disturbances, which express the truth that God's judgment on the Edomites is written in heaven. The destruction of the heavens is not meant 'literally'—if it were, there would hardly be a time 'from generation to generation' when the hawk and the porcupine could possess the ruins of Edom.

The next chapter, by contrast, looks forward to the paradisal regeneration of the desert, probably the Judaean wilderness, and the return to Zion of all the dispersed of Israel. It is easy to read the chapters as two sides of the same coin: Yahweh's judgment on the nations means prosperity for Israel. The theme of the desert is common to the two chapters. Edom becomes a wilderness, but the wilderness of Israel blossoms; Edom's streams of water turn to pitch (34.9), but for Israel even the dry places become pools and swamps (35.6-7). For this reason commentators nearly all agree that the two chapters form a unity, a kind of diptych.

This is supported by considerations of date. Anti-Edom oracles proliferate from the exilic period onwards, probably because of Edomite involvement in the sack of Jerusalem in 587—described in Obadiah 11-14, cf. Lam. 4.21. Isaiah 34 can hardly be earlier than this. (Before the exile Edom/Esau is treated as a 'brother' to Israel/Jacob.) Isaiah 35 similarly cannot be pre-exilic. It is extraordinarily similar in tone and style to Isaiah 40–55. It would be easy to imagine an edition of Isaiah lacking 36–39, the stories of Isaiah and Hezekiah, and then Isaiah 35 would run straight into Isaiah 40. It is a useful exercise to ask whether, if this were so, we should ever have come to the conclusion that Isaiah 35 was the work of anyone but Deutero-Isaiah. It would certainly not stand out as very different. As it is, however, commentators have usually seen the chapter as 'deutero-deutero-Isaianic', much like Isaiah 56–66: the work of a disciple, close in time but probably already back in Judah, rather than, like Deutero-Isaiah himself, still in Babylon awaiting the return. Isa. 35.10, it should be noted, is a quotation from Isa. 51.11—which implies that the author of Isaiah 35 knew Deutero-Isaiah's work, and hence wrote at a later time. Clements argues, additionally, that the verse is here used to predict the return of all the Jewish diaspora, whereas Deutero-Isaiah had only the Babylonian exiles in mind. If this is so, it supports a later date for Isaiah 35, though it has to be said that the latter point is not self-evidently true; for Deutero-Isaiah also speaks of the return of those from north, south, east and west (Isa. 43.5-7). But the balance of probability may be just in favour of seeing Isaiah 35 as modelled on the work of Deutero-Isaiah, rather than as part of it.

Thus these two chapters do make good sense in the same period, and succeed in imagining disaster and restoration with equal vividness and skill. Without being able to demonstrate the contrary, I do not feel entirely convinced that they were written to go together. Though the Exile is the earliest probable date for Isaiah 34, it is quite hard to show that it cannot be later, even much later. The full-blooded apocalyptic imagery would be easily compatible with a later date. What is more, whereas Isaiah 35 is so like Deutero-Isaiah that it could even be by him, Isaiah 34 seems to me not like him at all, nor like Trito-Isaiah. Once the chapters are juxtaposed, the parallels noted above are certainly striking, but if they were not juxtaposed, it is difficult to imagine that anyone would suggest bringing them together on the strength of the supposed similarities.

Perhaps this is to be too sceptical about the unity of these chapters. The reader will by now have seen that the consensus of modern scholarship on Isaiah tends in a unitary direction. It does not, indeed, try to defend wholly Isaianic authorship, like an older conservatism. But it is alert for signs of connection between chapters, and is inclined to reject the idea that the book's composition was in some way an accident. I do not wish to argue that this is mistaken, but to make sure that the student of Isaiah does not take the unity for granted too readily.

Whatever the origin of the 'Little Apocalypse', its contribution to chs. 1–39 is to focus attention on Israel's eschatological hope. The punishment of the nations, and the gathering in of the dispersed, are two major parts of the future for which post-exilic Jews looked and hoped. It may well be that the redactors who placed these oracles here were trying (as with 24–27) to generalize Isaiah's message and make it apply to their own time, perhaps to all times. The Little Apocalypse also makes a transition to the salvation oracles of Deutero-Isaiah, encouraging the reader to see the book of Isaiah as a seamless whole (which it is not).

The Historical Chapters (Isaiah 36–39)

In Chapter 1 above I mentioned the possible explanations for the origin of these chapters, which substantially duplicate the account of the 'Assyrian crisis' in 2 Kings 18–19. In principle the compiler of Isaiah could have copied them from Kings, the compiler of Kings could have copied them from Isaiah, or both could have taken them from a common source. There has been a lengthy and intricate scholarly debate on these options, which may be studied in the works of Clements, Smelik and Gonçalves listed at the end of the chapter. But however that question is resolved, anyone studying the redaction of Isaiah 1–39 is bound to ask what was the editor's intention in placing these chapters just here. If we regard ch. 35 as originally leading straight into Deutero-Isaiah (see above), then this later redactional decision has spoiled the effect of the earlier one. On the other hand, 36–39 taken as a whole have the interesting effect of charting not only the miraculous deliverance of Jerusalem but also the complacency to which this eventually led—making Hezekiah willing to open his secret treasuries to the envoys from Babylon (ch. 39). That for the author was the first fatal step on the road that led Hezekiah's descendants into their Babylonian exile, just over a century later. In the very next chapter of the book of Isaiah (ch. 40), Babylon is where we find the prophet and his audience, awaiting deliverance by God. These chapters thus bridge the gap between 'First' and 'Second' Isaiah.

This interpretation has a slightly subversive effect. One of the arguments critical scholars used, in the days when the existence of more than one 'Isaiah' was contentious, was that 40–55 concerned itself with the exiles in Babylon, and therefore could not be by Isaiah ben Amoz: there was a clear break between 1–39 and 40–55. Conservative scholars commonly retorted that the break had been created by ignoring 36–39. If these were read as a continuous part of the work, then the transition from Judah to Babylon was prepared for in the narrative. Prepared for, too, in Isaiah's mind: having grasped the terrible implications of Hezekiah's carelessness over the Babylonian envoys, he foresaw the exile to which it would eventually lead, and then uttered oracles about the eventual deliverance from exile. There are many reasons why most scholars did not find this convincing. But in so far as the case for Deutero-Isaiah rested on the perception of a *break* between 1–39 and 40–55, what we have just suggested about the rather smooth redaction at this point may seem to undermine it. Redaction criticism can be a dangerous ally.

Even if we remain convinced (as most scholars do) that there are indeed two (or three) 'Isaiahs', there is much to learn from noticing how the editor has collapsed the Assyrian crisis into the Babylonian one, ignoring the hundred years' gap. For the editors of the prophetic books, chronology was not very important. What mattered much more was the pattern of divine activity which all historical events revealed. God's justice might come swiftly, cutting down the sinner in the very moment of the sin, or slowly, punishing Hezekiah's sin only in his children and grandchildren—but come it would. And his mercy might come sooner than looked for, or it might delay for generations, but its eventual arrival should never be in doubt. To us, probably, the unpredictable variation of pace in God's activity makes it seem fairly erratic, and this is a problem. But for the compilers of the prophetic books, such variation was trivial, if only the controlling pattern stayed the same. On that basis the transition from Isaiah 39 to Isaiah 40 is far smoother than modern readers feel it to be.

Other Secondary Passages

It is not possible to comment on every non-Isaianic passage in Isaiah 1–39, but a few may be noted.

Isaiah 12

This serves as a doxological conclusion to Isaiah 1–11, and here we are again confronted with a familiar choice: is this a psalm which already existed, perhaps was even used in worship, or is it a redactional composition which never existed outside its present context? Clements favours the latter, and many commentators would agree. Indeed, it can be seen as a deliberate continuation of 11.12-16, yet another prophecy of the return of the dispersed and of the restoration of Israelite sovereignty over the land. This could lead naturally enough into a psalm of thanksgiving.

H.G.M. Williamson has suggested that 11.12-16 is meant to round off 6–11, as 5.26-30 rounds off 1–5 (note that each begins with the picture of Yahweh 'raising a flag'). Isa. 5.26-30 invites us to see Isaiah 1–5 as threatening Yahweh's judgment, 11.12-16 treats Isaiah 6–11 as promising salvation after the judgment. Isa. 12.1 then sums up both:

> I will give thanks to thee, O LORD,
>> for though thou wast angry with me,
> thy anger turned away,
>> and thou didst comfort me.

Thus the redactor encourages us to read Isaiah's message as being about judgment *followed by* salvation—and neither without the other.

On the other hand, it would be possible to take Isaiah 12 as containing two small psalms (1-2 and 4-6) which appealed to the redactor as apt, but which he did not invent. Verse 3 ('With joy you will draw water from the wells of salvation') might suggest a liturgical setting for at least the second of them. The characteristically Isaianic 'Holy One of Israel', however, occurs in this second passage, and it is very rare in the other psalms known to us. 'The Lord GOD is my strength and my song', on the other hand, echoes Exod. 15.2 and Ps. 118.4. Probably the balance is in favour of seeing all these passages as specially composed for their present place, but the case is weaker with Isaiah 12 than with the oracles in 5.24-30 and 11.12-16. But in any case it is clear that 1–12 has been ordered so as to present an alternation of punishment and blessing for Israel, with blessing as the last word. And this is consistent with what we have found in other parts of Isaiah 1–39.

Isaiah 32–33

These chapters consist of a variety of oracles, probably from different dates. Isa. 32.9-14 could perhaps be authentic, with its theme of the complacency of the women of Jerusalem—cf. 3.16-26. But what follows, with its prophecy of the outpouring of God's Spirit, must surely belong to the Persian period at the earliest, like Joel 2.28-29. Perhaps vv. 9-20 form a single prophecy, in which case they speak of judgment followed by salvation in the now familiar way.

The earlier part of ch. 32, vv. 1-8, can be read as a prediction of a coming king, either in realistic or in 'messianic' terms, and in that case it would generally be given a post-exilic date. But by v. 6 it has turned to general, rather timeless comments about the 'fool' in a way reminiscent of Proverbs. It may be that even the opening verses should be understood in this way—rendering v. 1, for instance, 'A king reigns by righteousness, and princes rule in justice', and taking them as a description of the ideal monarch and his reign—cf. Wis. 1.1-5. Such a little treatise on good kingship might come from almost any period. H. Barth sees the passage as belonging to the 'Josianic redaction' of Isaiah 1–39. Prophecies about disasters caused by various kings of Judah (28–31) thus conclude with a presentation of the ideal king. Indeed, Barth thinks that the rest of the chapter belongs to the same redactional stage, extending the vision of the perfect king into that of the renewed kingdom. If we could be sure that this chapter was once the end of a particular collection, we could agree that it does the job very well; as Clements says, 'it provides a very beautiful and fitting conclusion to the message of Isaiah, and looks to the future as a time of peace, security and general well-being'. But this must remain speculation. Certainly the style is unlike anything else in Isaiah 1–39, except for the following chapter.

This chapter, Isaiah 33, is also quite complex. Again,

vv. 14-16 have a 'wisdom' flavour, like 32.1-8, and vv. 17-22 present a memorable picture of a restored Zion, drawing probably on Isa. 54.1-3. It is a relief to know that 'no galley with oars' (presumably meaning a warship) will be able to sail past the new Jerusalem, though rather startling to find this stated as though it were unexpected. All in all the passage seems post-exilic, but Kaiser's Maccabean dating is, like all such very late datings, at risk from the argument that by the Maccabean age the book of Isaiah already existed as a finished whole, as attested by Ben Sira (Sir. 48.22-25). (Against this it could fairly be said that we do not know Ben Sira's Isaiah contained *precisely* what is in the book as we now have it.) An exilic date (thus Barth) is attractive, making this yet another part of Isaiah 1–39 not far removed in time from Deutero-Isaiah. And, in this resembling the Apocalypse of 24–27, it may draw on earlier Isaianic oracles and reverse them: compare, for example, 33.19 ('the people of an obscure speech which you cannot understand') with 28.11 ('by men of strange lips and with an alien tongue').

As a whole the chapter is often treated as a 'prophetic liturgy', containing a lament (vv. 7-9), a Torah-liturgy (vv. 14-16) and an oracle of salvation (vv. 17-24). But few commentators think the material was actually *used* liturgically. Rather, the redactor of Isaiah 1–39 has shaped this purely literary section after a liturgical model. I am inclined to think that attempts to discover when and why it was introduced into the book, and which earlier collection if any it rounded off, are likely to be a hopeless quest. But a satisfactory and convincing answer would be very welcome.

The Redaction of Isaiah 1–39

If nineteenth-century scholarship sometimes made it seem that the book of Isaiah was almost a random collection of prophecies with nothing in common, more recently the pendulum has swung in the opposite direction. Most scholars now think of Isaiah 1–39, indeed of the whole book of Isaiah, as a carefully crafted whole. Though some of the non-Isaianic sections may have begun life as anonymous oracles, once they were claimed for Isaiah their placing and exact wording (it is maintained) was given very careful thought. And comparatively few of the secondary oracles did have an independent existence: many of them, it is now thought, are the work of the redactors, and they were designed to produce just the effect they now do. Many were composed to change the direction of the earlier material, relativizing its words of judgment by adding prophecies of eventual salvation, or generalizing Isaiah's words about Judah under Ahaz into comments on the human race as a whole. The overall effect is to produce a book very much less rooted in the particularities of the eighth century and more open to constant reuse in the changing circumstances of any and every age.

I have sometimes sounded a cautionary note, and urged that we should not overlook the possibility that some oracles, or their location in the book, owe as much to chance as to planning. Nevertheless recent scholarship really has redrawn our map of this most complex of prophetic books, and redaction criticism has shown that it is coherent despite the complexity. In the final chapter we shall look at recent 'readings' of Isaiah 1–39. As we shall see, it is often felt nowadays that a reading of the 'final form' of Isaiah shows more respect for the text than the 'fragmentative' approach of older critical scholarship. Whether this is so or not, historical scholarship in any case has a duty to consider the present form of Isaiah 1–39. This is not so much because the text in that form does now exist and has a claim on our interpretative skills—the point commonly made today on behalf of the Bible 'as literature'—but because it is the version of Isaiah 1–39 that did, historically, exist in whatever period saw it completed. If we are interested in what Isaiah said, or in what the authors of later sections like 24–27 or 13–23 wrote, it also makes sense to be interested in what the final redactors were seeking to convey.

In *The Book Called Isaiah*, H.G.M. Williamson offers a theory about the reaction of Isaiah 1–55 which greatly simplifies the many complicated hypotheses on offer about this complex book. While accepting that it contains much material from diverse periods, he suggests that its compiler was the figure we know as Deutero-Isaiah. There never was a 'Book of Deutero-Isaiah'—that is, chs. 40–55 never existed as an independent work. Instead, a prophet living during the Exile edited and supplemented the existing book of Isaiah, and added to it sixteen further chapters, our present chs. 40–55. Much of the editorial material in 1–39 is thus intended to interpret Isaiah's oracles 'deutero-Isaianically', as we might say. Taken as a whole, Isaiah 1–55 is a work of the exilic age, intended by its compiler to convey, both through its revisions of older prophecies and its presentation of new ones, a unified message about God's punishment of his disobedient people and his eventual restoration of them. And this time of restoration, so Deutero-Isaiah believed, was now at hand. Williamson writes,

> I have argued for three main proposals in the course of this book, namely, (i) that Deutero-Isaiah was especially influenced by the literary deposit of Isaiah of Jerusalem...(ii) that he regarded the earlier work as in some sense a book that had been sealed up until the time when judgment should be past and the day of salvation had arrived, which day he believed himself to be heralding...and (iii) that in order to locate his message in relation to the earlier and continuing ways of God with Israel he included a version of the earlier prophecies with his own and edited them in such a way as to bind the two parts of the work together. (*The Book called Isaiah*, pp. 240-41)

The first of these points is as important as the other two in understanding the implications of Williamson's theory. It is not as if Deutero-Isaiah took just any collection of old prophecies and attached to them his own words, forcing an alien meaning into them. Deutero-Isaiah's own prophetic message was crucially dependent on the words of Isaiah of Jerusalem, and shares many themes in common with the eighth-century figure. In attaching his own words to Isaiah's he was not seeking to twist Isaiah's message into the likeness of his own, but to update it and to create a harmonious whole from the combination of his own message and that of his predecessor. This is a sophisticated redactional theory, which has (among other positive points) the merit of accounting for both continuity and discontinuity within the book of Isaiah.

In the next chapter we shall see that some scholars are now urging a 'holistic' reading of Isaiah, ignoring the alleged stratification of the book painstakingly investigated by historical critics. Williamson's hypothesis neatly bridges the divide between such 'final-form' readings and an interest in the book's historical growth. Against proponents of reading the book piecemeal, he wants to see 1–55 as a single unit, with a coherent 'message'. But on the other hand, the unity and coherence of these chapters is not something we, the modern readers, simply *decide* to impose on them. At the point where 1–55 first came to exist as a whole, they *were* unified and coherent, through the deliberate intention of the prophet we call Deutero-Isaiah. In this case at least, the now common distinction between 'historical' and 'literary' reading of texts—the former interested in details of how the texts came to be, the latter interested only in the finished product—is clearly an oversimplification.

As further studies appear of the redaction history of other prophetic books, it should become possible to give a much fuller account of the development of Jewish theological thought, especially where eschatology is concerned, in the Second Temple period. If the books attributed to the pre-exilic prophets were put together deliberately and methodically, rather than in the haphazard way assumed by some earlier scholars, then in their present form they are good evidence for religious thought in the period when they were compiled, just as much as the authentic words of the named prophet are evidence for the thought of his day. If the final edition of Isaiah 1–39 was, as Kaiser thinks, a work of the Maccabean age (early second century), then we ought to study it synoptically with the book of Daniel; if it comes from the mid-Persian period (say late fifth to early fourth century), then we need to consider it alongside Chronicles, Ezra and Nehemiah; and if Williamson is right, and these chapters were carefully worked over and supplemented by Deutero-Isaiah, they should be read in the context of his work and of the other rich theological works produced during the Exile. 'Final form exegesis' has an important *historical* task in front of it, irrespective of how it fares in the literary arena.

Further Reading

On the oracles against the nations, see

O. Kaiser, *Isaiah 13–39* (London: SCM Press, 1974; 2nd edn 1980).
S. Erlandsson, *The Burden of Babylon (A Study of Isaiah 13.2–14.23)* (ConBOT, 4; Lund: Gleerup, 1970).
R.B.Y. Scott, 'Isaiah XXI.1-10: The Inside of a Prophet's Mind', *VT* 2 (1952), pp. 278-82.
A. Macintosh, *Isaiah XXI: A Palimpsest* (Cambridge: Cambridge University Press, 1980).

On the Isaiah Apocalypse, see Kaiser, above.

On Isaiah 36–39, see

*R.E. Clements, *Isaiah and the Deliverance of Jerusalem: A Study of the Interpretation of Prophecy in the Old Testament* (JSOTSup 13; Sheffield: JSOT Press, 1980).
—'The Prophecies of Isaiah and the Fall of Jerusalem in 587 BC', *VT* 30 (1980), pp. 421-36.
K.A.D. Smelik, 'Distortion of Old Testament Prophecy: The Purpose of Isaiah xxxvi and xxxvii', *OTS* 24 (1986), pp. 70-93.
C.R. Seitz, *Zion's Final Destiny: The Development of the Book of Isaiah—A Reassessment of Isaiah 36–39* (Minneapolis: Fortress Press, 1991).

On Isaiah 32–33, see

J.J.M. Roberts, 'Isaiah 33: An Isaianic Elaboration of the Zion Tradition', in C.L. Meyers and M. O'Connor (eds.), *The Word of the Lord Shall Go Forth* (FS D.N. Freedman; Winona Lake, IN: Eisenbrauns, 1983), pp. 15-25.

On the reworking of old prophecies in new situations, see

*R.P. Carroll, *When Prophecy Failed: Reactions and Responses to Failure in the Old Testament Prophetic Tradition* (London: SCM Press, 1979).

On the redaction of Isaiah, see

R.E. Clements, 'Beyond Tradition History: Deutero-Isaianic Development of First Isaiah's Themes', *JSOT* 31 (1985), pp. 45-113.
*—'The Unity of the Book of Isaiah', *Int* 36 (1982), pp. 117-29.
H.G.M. Williamson, *The Book Called Isaiah: Deutero-Isaiah's Role in Composition and Redaction* (Oxford: Oxford University Press, 1994).
M.A. Sweeney, *Isaiah 1–4 and the Post-Exilic Understanding of the Isaianic Tradition* (BZAW, 171; Berlin: Töpelmann, 1988).

Other works referred to:

J. Vermeylen, *Du prophète Isaïe à l'apocalyptique* (2 vols.; Paris, 1977).

G. Fohrer, *Das Buch Jesaja* (3 vols.; Stuttgart: Zwingli Verlag, 1962–64).

—'Der Aufbau der Apokalypse des Jesajabuchs (Isa. 24–27)', *CBQ* (1963), pp. 34-56; survey of possible analyses of the Isaiah Apocalypse.

J. Lindblom, *Die Jesaja-Apokalypse: Jes. 24–27* (Lund, 1938); classic study of the Isaiah Apocalypse.

H. Barth, *Die Jesaja-Worte in der Josiazeit* (WMANT, 48; Neukirchen–Vluyn: Neukirchener Verlag, 1977); argues for a major redaction of Isaiah's oracles in the reign of Josiah.

M.L. Henry, *Glaubenskrise und Glaubensbewährung in den Dichtungen der Jesajaapokalypse* (BWANT, 86; Stuttgart, 1967); an early post-exilic date for Isaiah 24–27.

O.H. Steck, *Bereitete Heimkehr: Jesaja 35 als redaktionelle Brücke zwischen dem Ersten und dem Zweiten Jesaja* (SBS, 121; Stuttgart, 1985); sees Isaiah 35 as written to connect 1–34 and 40–55, which already existed as separate works.

J. Vermeylen, 'L'unité du livre d'Isaïe', in *The Book of Isaiah* (BETL, 81; Leuven: Leuven University Press, 1989), pp. 11-53.

F.J. Gonçalves, *L'expédition de Sennachérib en Palestine dans la littérature hébraïque ancienne* (EB, ns, 7; Paris, 1986); detailed investigation of Isaiah 36–39 and parallels in Kings.

A.E. Cowley, *Aramaic Papyri of the Fifth Century BC* (Oxford: Clarendon Press, 1923); evidence of Jewish life in Egypt.

6

READING ISAIAH

Until recently it was unusual to suggest that Isaiah 1–39 ought to be read as a whole, still less that the whole book of Isaiah should be. People who rejected 'critical' biblical scholarship did indeed suggest this, since the book of Isaiah really was, in their view, the work of the prophet Isaiah ben Amoz. But it is only in the last few years that critical scholars have also come to be interested in the 'final form', as it is usually called, of the book. Since this is a study of Isaiah 1–39, I shall not say much about attempts to reintegrate chs. 40–66 into the book; but inevitably interest has not stopped at the end of ch. 39. Some of the current theories about the 'final form' can be applied, however, to the 'semi-final' document, chs. 1–39. The division between 1–39 and 40–66 is in any case regarded, by almost everyone, as the sharpest in the book.

In Chapter 1 above we considered various theories about how the book of Isaiah came into its present form. Two main models seem to be used: a school of disciples, reworking and supplementing the words of the prophet over a period of years or even centuries (Eaton, Jones, Mowinckel, Vermeylen); or groups of scribes, editing the books of the prophets in much the same way as they edited the books of the Torah or, indeed, other ancient works (Perlitt, Fishbane, Fohrer).

In the last chapter we looked in more detail at some theories about the composition of various post-Isaianic sections, and saw that there is evidence for a sixth-century edition of

'Isaiah' in the time of Deutero-Isaiah (around 540 BC).
H.G.M. Williamson has made a detailed study of this stage in
the redaction. In the seventh century there had already been
a 'Josianic redaction', according to the theory of Hermann
Barth.

Both these redactions, in the seventh and sixth centuries
respectively, seem to have involved what look like features of
both the models just mentioned. Without transmission by
disciples of the prophet, it is hard to see how Isaiah's oracles
would have been available for editing. Yet the editing
depended on a knowledge of the written form of the text, and
it set considerable store by precise verbal nuances and the
order of the oracles—which tend to be arranged so that predictions of weal and of woe alternate. If Williamson is right,
for example, chs. 1–12 falls into two halves, the first (1–5)
focusing on disaster, the second (6–11) on restoration, with
ch. 12 as a doxological conclusion to the whole. In the end the
two models are not incompatible; for the scribes who edited
Isaiah presumably felt an allegiance to his words and his
memory, and the disciples who initially handed them down
must have been able to write (unless we adopt a full-blown
'oral tradition' view of the matter).

Literary Readings of Isaiah

Modern discussion of the redactional history of Isaiah tends
to assume greater continuity between the prophet and the
book that bears his name than did nineteenth-century critics,
who often emphasized the negative point that this or that
section could not be by the prophet himself. To that extent
the older, sharp division between 'critical' and 'pre-critical'
scholarship has been softened. Later stages in the growth of
the book are, it would still be stressed, very different in their
message from anything Isaiah himself would have said, yet
they remain in some perceptible continuity with his own
words and ideas. It is important to see that commentators
who are very ready to treat important chapters of Isaiah
1–39 as 'inauthentic' may at the same time have a high view
of this continuity. Vermeylen, for instance, regards vast
tracts of Isaiah 1–39 as secondary—including even such 'core'

oracles as the 'Song of the Vineyard' (5.1-7). Yet at the same time he believes that the final message of Isaiah 1–39 retains much from the themes of the prophet's own preaching. Isaiah himself, like the book named after him, balanced a foreboding of the inevitable downfall of Judah with the belief that Yahweh's care for his people knew no end and would eventually prevail. This paradox of judgment and grace still pervades the whole book in its final form, and is the reason for its bewildering swings from despair to joy, epitomized in ch. 12 or in chs. 34–35.

This way of looking at the book as a finished whole is perhaps best called 'literary', in that it tries to read Isaiah not as a *document* from the past, full of rewritings and insertions, but as a literary *work*—much as we read novels or plays, taking their unity as a given. Such a reading may well take seriously the presence of dissonant elements in Isaiah, and fully accept that these mean the book cannot have originated as a single entity, composed by one prophet. But the disparate materials from which the work is composed have none the less been drawn together in such a way that the resulting book is much more than a collection of fragments—the whole is greater than the sum of its parts. By paying attention to the subtleties of the text, it is possible, and desirable, to read Isaiah as a unity. Taken together, and with the order imposed on them by the redactors, all the oracles attributed to Isaiah 'make sense': they are a book, not a mere folder full of rough drafts and collected scraps.

Canonical Criticism

This literary interest in the book of Isaiah as a finished whole happens to have arisen at a time when other scholars are promoting unitary readings of biblical books for quite different reasons. Since the 1970s some biblical scholars have advanced theological, rather than literary, reasons why Isaiah (or any other book of the Bible) should be read as a whole, not dissected and atomized. Such thinking is generally described as 'canonical criticism'. The title is rather misleading, since it unites two different programmes, those of B.S. Childs and J.A. Sanders. Oversimplifying, it can be said that Childs has been more concerned with the 'canonical form' of scriptural texts, that is, the form they had at the point where Jews and Christians 'canonized' them. Sanders's interest focuses more on the process by which this canonical form developed. But many biblical scholars have been influenced by both Childs and Sanders, and would want to ascribe a high value both to Isaiah as we now have it and to the process by which it came into existence.

What is more, an interest in the Bible as the church's (or the synagogue's) book has restored for many the importance of traditional Jewish and Christian interpretation (see J. Sawyer's discussion in *From Moses to Patmos*). It is sometimes argued nowadays that a 'canonical' approach can undo the harm allegedly done to Jewish and Christian use of Scripture by the historical-critical method, while continuing to affirm that method as valid in its own limited sphere. Whether this is so or not, such a high claim serves to confirm that the reading of Isaiah as a unity is firmly on the agenda of scholarship today.

What does Isaiah (or Isa. 1–39) 'mean', if read in a unitary way? Edgar W. Conrad's recent book *Reading Isaiah* makes the interesting suggestion that the key to Isaiah as it now stands is its reference to the future. However minor a theme messianic hopes are in the original message of the prophet Isaiah, as it stands the book is orientated firmly towards the future:

> The Book of Isaiah (chs. 1–66) provides the context and occasion for reading another book, the book of Isaiah's vision (chs. 6–39). The book is structured in such a way as to provide a present context as the framework (chs. 1–5 and 40–66) for the reception of the ancient vision of Isaiah (chs. 6–39)...
>
> The vision of Isaiah was an alien text at the time of its inception because in its own time it was a book written for another time, a future time. Only after Isaiah's time could the vision of Isaiah be read with understanding (pp. 155-56).

Possibly implied here is the thought that it has been rather perverse of critical scholarship to spend so much time relocating Isaiah in his own time, when the aim of the book's 'final form' is to move his oracles into the future and see them as intended for readers of a much later time! Whether that is so or not, there is much to be said for Conrad's idea that the community which produced and canonized the book of Isaiah thought of the prophet as having spoken deliberately obscure oracles (cf. 6.9-10, 29.10-12), which had no contemporary reference but were to be treasured up till a time in the future when they would find their fulfilment—cf. Dan. 9.2, 24; 10.14; and see my *Oracles of God.*

Childs's verdict on the meaning of Isaiah as a finished text emphasizes far less its application to one specific future time, the 'age of salvation', and much more its general applicability. For example, the mixing of oracles from many different periods—Assyrian, Babylonian, and Persian—serves to decontextualize *all* of them. The reader is meant to draw general theological instruction from the oracles which is not time-bound or culture-specific. By joining oracles about Cyrus (in chs. 40–55) to oracles about the Assyrians (in 1–39), the editors (or canonizers) have sought to deflect the reader's interest away from both Cyrus and Sennacherib and on to the general idea of pretended human, as opposed to real divine, power. It might be said that, on Childs's interpretation, the prophecy of Isaiah turns into something a little like wisdom literature—insight into the human condition, applicable in every age equally. At any rate a comparison of Childs's reading with Conrad's can only help to emphasize how varied are the conclusions that can be reached by two interpreters both committed to the 'final form' of the text as the proper basis for exegesis.

Themes in Isaiah 1–39

Even if we choose not to commit ourselves to these deliberately unitary readings, it is possible to identify a number of themes that run through Isaiah 1–39 and explain in part the impression of unity that the book makes even on casual readers. The fact that these themes occur in both 'authentic' and 'secondary' material may slightly support the idea of a 'school' of Isaiah—the secondary additions are mostly not, for example, close in theme to Jeremiah or Ezekiel. Yet from a historical-critical perspective the themes are often given a rather different treatment in the secondary passages from the one they receive in the oracles of Isaiah himself. So what follows provides support both for theories of a coherent redaction of Isaiah 1–39, and also for an analysis which stresses the book's stratification and complex compositional history. There is no reason why the reader of Isaiah should not believe in both.

The Holy One of Israel

Since one of the distinguishing marks of the Old Testament is that all the literature it contains is religious, it is hardly surprising that every strand or layer in Isaiah 1–39 is about God. However, God is not conceptualized in exactly the same way in all the Old Testament books, and it is striking that there seems definitely to be an 'Isaianic' picture of him, which to some extent cuts across the source-divisions in the book. Most readers notice the phrase 'the Holy One of Israel', but may not realize how specific this is to Isaiah. It occurs twelve times in 1–39 and eleven in 40–55 (only twice in 56–66), but hardly at all elsewhere in the Old Testament. In form it corresponds to the titles of God in Genesis: the Shield of Abraham, the Mighty One of Jacob. These are often thought to be very old, originally perhaps the titles of different, tribal gods. It is possible that the same is true of 'the Holy One of Israel', and it could be mere accident that the name is preserved mostly in Isaiah. But if so, it is an odd coincidence that this is one of two prophetic books (the other is Ezekiel) where the *holiness* of God is most emphasized; and that Isaiah's inaugural vision, in ch. 6, is taken up with the theme of Yahweh's holiness. The seraphim describe him as 'Holy, Holy, Holy'; the prophet reacts by recalling the uncleanness of contemporary Judah, including himself. Whatever the original meaning of $q\bar{a}d\hat{o}\check{s}$, 'holy', may have been, Isaiah 6 treats it as implying the exaltedness of Yahweh above the created world, and his total 'cleanness'— his abhorrence of all pollution, both ritual and moral. Iniquity and corruption constitute 'despising the Holy One of Israel' in 1.4, as does rejection of his prophets' message in 30.11. God's holiness is manifested in his just judgment on sin (5.16).

Thus the essence of holiness for Isaiah seems to have been God's supremacy over everything, coupled with his total freedom from contamination with anything unclean or sinful: absolute power and absolute purity. We have already seen how important for Isaiah was the exalted character of Yahweh, the world sovereign whom no mortal should presume to challenge. This is why pride is so central to his understanding of human sin. Holiness, as he uses the term, precisely fits this concept of the divine nature. So while possible, it does not seem probable that the title 'Holy One of Israel' occurs by accident in his oracles rather than in those of other prophets.

This makes the proportionally even more frequent occurrence in 40–55 rather remarkable, and may well support the view that 1–39 and 40–55 have a more than casual connection. Indeed, not only the term, but also the underlying theological idea, does seem to be common to the two collections. The exaltedness of the God of Israel, by contrast with the 'idols' worshipped by other nations, is much stressed by Deutero-Isaiah: 'To whom will you compare me, that I should be like him? says the Holy One' (Isa. 40.25). And God's holiness implies that his worshippers must be free from all that would contaminate them (52.11). Deutero-Isaiah seems to have a distinctly 'Isaianic' view of God—explicable if he was in some sense a disciple, or at least was strongly influenced by the eighth-century prophet, as Williamson argues. Williamson's hypothesis that Deutero-Isaiah edited 1–39 does of course raise the opposite possibility—that holiness is a term from Deutero-Isaiah's vocabulary, unsurprising in a contemporary of Ezekiel, and that its prominence in the oracles of Isaiah himself is due to Deutero-Isaiah's editorial hand. But the centrality of the theme in Isaiah 6, marking the prophet's understanding of his mission and of the one who had called him to it from the very beginning, makes it preferable to think that this is indeed an idea we owe to Isaiah himself. That is not to say that all occurrences in 1–39 are 'authentic'. Interestingly, the psalm in ch. 12 concludes (12.6), 'Shout, and sing for joy, O inhabitant of Zion, for great in your midst is the Holy One of Israel'. Thus 1–12, one of the major earlier collections in the book, finishes with this characteristically Isaianic theme. It stresses that the coming restoration of Israel is an expression of the exaltedness of

Yahweh, the Holy One, a point on which Isaiah, Deutero-Isaiah, and most of the other contributors to the book would surely have agreed (cf. also 29.19). It is hard to avoid the conclusion that, whether deliberately or not, the book of Isaiah has been drawn together into a unity through the controlling theme of God's holiness. A careful reading needs to do justice both to the different nuances that the concept acquires in the different contexts and periods of the book's composition, and to the remarkable unity it imparts to the book. It is not at all surprising that many readers perceive it as quite a unified work, for all its complexity.

Israel

So far we have asked what the title 'Holy One of Israel' tells us about the concept of God in the book of Isaiah. But the word 'Israel' itself is no less interesting. 'Israel' appears, historically, to have been the name of the northern kingdom, with its capital at Samaria. But Isaiah scarcely ever uses it in this sense: when the northern kingdom is mentioned, it is usually called 'Ephraim' (7.2, 8-9; 9.9, 21; 11.12-13; 17.3; 28.1, 3; for an exceptional use of 'Israel' for the north, see 9.8).

'Israel' (sometimes also 'Jacob') seems, for Isaiah, to be usually a religious term, meaning something like 'the people of Yahweh'. This is why, confusingly for us, it can be used in oracles addressed to Judah, the southern kingdom (e.g. 1.3; 5.7), or to both kingdoms understood as two parts of Yahweh's 'people' (e.g. 'both houses of Israel', 8.14). Although Isaiah has the political realities of life in Palestine sharply in focus, he does not regard the present political arrangements as any kind of index of the true relationship between Yahweh and this particular portion of the human race. 'Israel' in principle includes the northern kingdom as well as Judah, even if that kingdom has perished (in 721 BC); on the other hand, if only Judah, or even (as in 701 BC) only Jerusalem is left intact, then all the demands Yahweh makes on 'Israel' rightly fall on that city, however small a fragment it is of the whole people.

Thus to belong to 'Israel' is not to have a merely political identity; it is to be part of a group of people constituted by its relationship to Yahweh, and having a particular answerability to him. This comes out nowhere so clearly as in the Song of the Vineyard (5.1-7): the house of Israel is Yahweh's prized vineyard, and in return for the care he has lavished on it it ought to bear 'good grapes'—which is a metaphor for justice and righteousness. Or, in another image (1.2), Israel is like a family of sons brought up by their father, Yahweh, who have become disobedient and thankless.

This idea of what it was to be 'Israel' is so familiar to modern Bible readers that we tend not to notice how odd it is. The names of nations can indeed turn into metaphors for the qualities those nations are supposed to exemplify. 'There'll always be an England' means, not that England in the literal sense will never cease to exist (we have to turn to 'Rule, Britannia' for that), but that the quintessence of Englishness is somehow indestructible. Wherever cricket is played, beer is warm, and rain soaks newly-mown grass, England will have survived. But it may be doubted whether this idea would in fact go on being asserted if there really were, in the physical sense, no England at all. The term 'Israel', however, far outlasted its original and uncomplicated political use. For many centuries, following the Roman destruction of Jerusalem in the first century of our era, until the founding of the modern State of Israel, it applied to Jews—Yahweh's people—irrespective of the fact that they had no unified political identity. Isaiah is at the beginning of this development, and though he does not use the term very often, it is important to see the far-reaching implications when he does.

Should we say that this use of the term 'Israel' implies the idea of the *covenant* between God and Israel? Isaiah never uses the word *berît*, the technical term for covenant. But if we understand the covenant to mean that there is a special relationship between Yahweh and the group/people/nation that called itself Israel, Jacob, or Ephraim and Judah, and that this relationship involved mutual obligations, then certainly the idea was there even if the term was not. We should be wary, however, of extrapolating much further from this. Isaiah shows little interest in what Old Testament scholars call the 'saving history' of Israel, as recorded in the Pentateuch. He nowhere mentions the lawgiving on Sinai,

nor does he speak about the Exodus, Moses, or the settlement of the Promised Land. His concept of 'Israel' embraces
all the descendants of Jacob in theory, but in practice he is
usually thinking of Jerusalem, its people and its traditions,
as the focus of Yahweh's concerns in the eighth century. We
cannot know, therefore, that he was thinking of the
'covenant' in the sense the term has in Exodus or
Deuteronomy. Perhaps, in fact, it was from Isaiah and other
similar teachers that those who formulated the official
account of the nation's history drew their inspiration, rather
than the other way around.

The successors of Isaiah who contributed so much of 1–39
certainly saw his use of 'Israel'—which they continued—as
implying the covenant and, with it, the sacred history. In
27.12 the people of Israel are to be gathered in, from
Mesopotamia and from Egypt, in a new Exodus, much like
the one foretold by Deutero-Isaiah (52.11-12). Mount Zion
and its inhabitants are to be protected by a 'cloud by day' and
'a flaming fire by night', just like the people who left Egypt
under Moses (cf. Exod. 13.21-22). God's law will be declared,
not only for Israel but for all nations, from Jerusalem (2.3).
At least in the 'Isaiah Apocalypse' (24–27) the word
'covenant' is used explicitly, though perhaps with reference
to a 'cosmic covenant', not merely the covenant made at Sinai
(24.5—cf. R. Murray). And 'Israel' is clearly an idealized 'people of God', even more so than in the authentic oracles of
Isaiah, and has the potential of spreading not just throughout Palestine but everywhere in the world: 'In days to come
Jacob shall take root, Israel shall blossom and put forth
shoots, and fill the whole world with fruit' (27.6). This, again,
is reminiscent of themes in Deutero-Isaiah (54.1-3; 55.5), and
may support the theory that 1–39 was edited at the time of
Deutero-Isaiah, if not actually edited by him.

There is thus a consistent idea of 'Israel', running through
various strata in Isaiah 1–39 and helping to bind the book
together. We might say that Isaiah and the book that now
bears his name share (a) a belief in the special vocation of
'Israel', (b) a dismay that it seems so little to have accepted
the obligations that go with this vocation, and yet also (c) a
(more or less) confident hope that God will honour his side of

the relationship, and eventually raise his people to greater prosperity than they have so far known. The detail of this set of convictions varied over the long period in which Isaiah 1–39 was growing, but the broad outlines remained remarkably constant.

King and Messiah

Isaiah has been the most important of the prophetic books for Christians seeking 'messianic' prophecies—not only the 'Immanuel' oracle of 7.10-14, but 'unto us a child is born' in 9.2-7, the 'shoot from the stump of Jesse' in 11.1-9, and the evocative passage beginning 'Your eyes will see the king in his beauty' in 33.17-22. The application of such oracles to Jesus has always been questioned by Jews, and in more recent times by many critical scholars, by asking the two questions (1) are these passages really messianic? and (2) if they are, can we know that it is Jesus Christ to whom they refer? The second question would take us outside the scope of this book. But the first can helpfully point us to the way Isaiah's message was gradually adapted and extended by the addition of later material, to produce a book that in this area too presents the modern reader with a surprisingly unified message.

The Messiah, as is generally agreed, was conceived in Judaism of the Second Temple period as a king of the line of David. The Davidic monarchy had ceased with the exile of Jehoiachin, the last legitimate king of Judah, in 598 BC. When some Jews returned from Babylonia in the 530s, there were some short-lived hopes that there would once more be a king. Some of these hopes may have centered on the governor Zerubbabel (see Ezra 5.1-2; Hag. 2.20-23; Zech. 4.1-10), who (though appointed by the Persians) was the grandson of Jehoiachin, and so had a defensible claim. In fact, however, nothing came of such hopes, and it was only in the second century BC that there were again 'kings' in Israel, the Hasmoneans—and they only in a limited sense. The hope for a king, detached from realistic fulfilment, was transmuted into a hope for a deliverer whom God himself would send in a more or less miraculous way. But the royal associations of the Messiah were never forgotten.

The oracles of Isaiah—those generally considered authentic—show that he had a closer association with the kings of Judah than any other prophet except, perhaps, Jeremiah. Whether or not he was a professional royal counsellor, as some think, he had easy access to the king and was able to approach him directly (7.1-17, cf. chs. 37 and 39). It would therefore not be surprising if he had prophesied about the king and his house—perhaps about future kings as well as the reigning monarch. If 9.2-7 is taken as the celebration of the current king (perhaps at his coronation, described as a symbolic new birth), or as the prediction of the birth of an heir, there is no reason why Isaiah should not be its author. If it is taken as messianic in a more strict sense, then there is a problem: would the prophet have foretold the coming of one to *restore* David's line at a time when that line was still unbroken and in possession of the royal city, Jerusalem?

The problem is analogous to that of the 'hopeful remnant' oracles. To hope for the restoration of a remnant makes sense if disaster has already struck and nothing but a remnant remains, but it seems unduly complicated if the nation is flourishing in any case. So with the 'messianic' oracles: logically we should have to say that Isaiah was foretelling first the collapse and then the miraculous restoration of the dynasty of David. This might have been a rather ambiguous message for his audience to assimilate, though obviously not an impossible one. Of course, if 9.2-7 is later than Isaiah and comes from a time when the dynasty *had* fallen—from the exilic age, for example—then it can be taken as messianic; though it might still be better to regard it as a realistic expression of the hopes that focused on Zerubbabel, or some other actual descendant of David.

However such passages are interpreted, it remains clear that they do constitute a body of material in Isaiah 1–39 which might be called 'royal/messianic'. They talk of kings, to an extent almost unparalleled in the prophets. The book of Isaiah is about the royal city, Jerusalem or 'Zion', about Judah, the state over which David's descendants ruled, and about the kings themselves, whether real or hoped for. The extensive material about the 'inviolability of Zion', which has already been discussed, can be seen as also related to the 'royal' theme (see Clements and Barth). Zion is the city David captured and made his personal possession, and its safety and the king's were closely bound up together (cf. Ps. 89, where king and city seem to blend into each other). The twin themes of the monarchy and the city of Zion emerge as clearly from post-Isaianic strata in 1–39 as from the authentic oracles of Isaiah himself. They are highlighted all the more by the absence, again from almost all strata, of what may be seen as the more typical or central Old Testament themes of Exodus, Moses, law and covenant. Though some later additions do introduce exodus themes (see above), they do not shift the weight of the book away from its unique emphasis on 'royal Zion'.

Zion is indeed a major theme of Deutero-Isaiah, which might lend further weight to Williamson's theory that he was the editor of Isaiah 1–39. But there is almost nothing about the king in 40–55 (only 55.3), and on this subject there is less continuity between the two major blocks of 1–39 and 40–55. Very striking is the prominence of the royal theme in 32–33, where the coming king is associated with marvellous fruitfulness (32.15-20) and security (33.17-22) in a way that can well be called 'messianic'. Zion, where the king lives, will in the future become a completely safe refuge, no longer at the mercy of foreign armies. As 14.32 puts it, 'What will one answer the messengers of the nation? "The Lord has founded Zion, and in her the afflicted of his people find refuge"'. If we read Isaiah 1–39 as a whole, this emerges as a major theme of the work.

Faith

A linchpin of Isaiah's political advice to the kings of Judah was the need for faith, *'emûnâ*—trust in God, steadfastness in loyalty to him, and refusal to pay enemies the compliment of being afraid of them. These rather complicated ideas were unpacked a little in Chapter 3. We saw that 'faith' is understood by Isaiah as the most appropriate way of responding to a God who is himself utterly reliable and completely trustworthy, but whose commitment to his people, though absolute, must not be presumed upon. As we have seen, 'faith', in the political sphere, is congruous with the virtues

Isaiah recognizes in matters of social morality: respect for those in authority, avoidance of self-assertion and pride, resistance to the temptation to make up one's own rules. It is a highly distinctive feature of Isaiah's message, worked out in a more thorough way than the moral categories used by other prophets.

When we begin to 'read Isaiah', we find that in this area too there is a marked family resemblance between the different parts of the book. For example, 30.15-17 is a classic statement of the faith theme in Isaiah of Jerusalem:

> For thus said the Lord God, the Holy One of Israel,
>   'In returning and rest you shall be saved;
>   in quietness and in trust shall be your strength'.
> And you would not, but you said,
> 'No! we will speed upon horses',
>   therefore you shall speed away...
> till you are left
>   like a flagstaff on the top of a mountain,
>   like a signal on a hill.

This is plainly a threat: lack of trust in God, seeking alliances with Egypt instead, has doomed the nation to destruction or at best serious defeat. In v. 18, however, a later editor has added a note of hope:

> Therefore the Lord waits to be gracious to you;
>   therefore he exalts himself to show mercy to you.
> For the Lord is a God of justice;
>   blessed are all those who wait for him.

Here are, essentially, the same themes. Yahweh waits patiently for the appropriate time to restore Israel (just as in 18.4 he waited for the moment to strike). His exalting himself is not a threat, but the best sign of hope: the exalted God is the one who can save. And the appropriate response for Judah is to wait in its turn—not to precipitate events, but to abide God's good time. Clements is probably right to see this as an exilic addition, giving a positive meaning to the empty space of the exile as the time of waiting for God to act (cf. Lam. 3.25-30). But the editor who added it had an extraordinarily 'Isaianic' mind.

The same is true of other secondary passages. Isaiah 32–33, which as we have seen may also be from the exilic

period, similarly uses Isaiah's themes of trust and patience
to encourage the readers to endure present troubles, in the
assurance that God will eventually intervene to save them:
'O Lord, be gracious to us; we wait for thee' (33.1). The rulers
appointed by God will be 'like a hiding place from the wind, a
covert from the tempest, like streams of water in a dry place,
like the shade of a great rock in a weary land' (32.2). God
himself will ensure that his people enjoy the peace and security of which these lovely images speak. When 'the Spirit is
poured out from on high', then

> justice will dwell in the wilderness,
> and righteousness abide in the fruitful field.
> And the effect of righteousness will be peace,
> and the result of righteousness, *quietness and trust* for ever.
> My people will abide in a peaceful habitation,
> in secure dwellings, and in quiet resting places (32.15-18).

When Isaiah said to the rulers of Judah, 'In returning and
in rest you shall be saved; in quietness and in trust shall be
your strength' (30.15), he was talking about political and military action. But his words are often appropriated by modern
Bible readers as a call for personal trust in the God who can
be relied on to uphold those who place themselves in his
hands. The book of Isaiah, in the form it now has, seems to
have already treated them in this way—not, perhaps, as part
of individual spirituality, but certainly as applying to the
whole mode of life of God's people. The God of Isaiah is a God
accessible only to those who accept him on his own terms and
leave all initiatives to him, and the book named after Isaiah
applies that insight in a range of different contexts.

Even the Isaiah Apocalypse (24–27), otherwise more distant than most of the additions from the themes of the
prophet himself, contributes one example: 'Thou dost keep
him in perfect peace, whose mind is stayed on thee, because
he trusts in thee. Trust in the LORD for ever, for the Lord
GOD is an everlasting rock' (26.3-4).

More than this, the whole ordering of the book presents a
regular pattern of divine activity in which God's punishment
of the people through military defeat is regularly followed by
restoration, encouraging patient endurance in the certain
hope of eventual deliverance. Once again this underlying

theme brings Isaiah 1–39 very close to 40–55, in which we read, 'for a brief moment I forsook you, but with great compassion I will gather you' (54.7). Isaiah 1–55 (and perhaps also 56–66), though they cannot easily be read as a unity, are nevertheless more than a mere anthology. There is a recognizably 'Isaianic' character to most of the material, and the themes of faith, reliability, trust, patience, endurance, and a kind of passivity weave in and out of these chapters, in authentic and secondary oracles alike.

Reading Isaiah 1–39

Can we read Isaiah 1–39? One of the impulses that led scholars to analyse these chapters with such care—sifting out genuine sayings of Isaiah ben Amoz from the many tangled additions made to them by later editors—was a feeling that 1–39 as it stands is actually 'unreadable'. By that is not meant that the book is *difficult* to read (as we may say that a novel we have just finished was 'not very readable'), nor, literally, that it is pure gibberish. To call 1–39 unreadable is to say that it does not cohere, that it creates no overall impression on the mind, that we lose the thread, or suspect there is no thread to lose. There are many coherent, 'readable', collections *within* 1–39, but the work as a whole makes no sense.

Until recently people who rejected this pessimistic judgment usually did so in the name of a conservative commitment to the Isaianic authorship of 1–39 (or indeed of 1–66). The book was all by one person, they argued, and so obviously must make overall sense; the defect was in scholars' sensitivity to Isaiah's message, not in the message itself. There still are defenders of the complete unity of Isaiah, but they are now rather few. Those who nowadays see Isaiah 1–39 as 'readable' usually do so not because they dispute the critical judgment that it is the result of a long process of development, but because they think that process was by no means so haphazard as earlier scholars asserted—or because they believe the finished product is in any case not nearly as chaotic as was once supposed. Either way, 1–39 emerges as an intelligible work, whose overall 'message' it makes sense to seek.

In this chapter I have tried to do justice to this recent shift of emphasis by drawing out a few themes that characterize the book of Isaiah as it stands, and also by paying some attention to the shape of the book and the implications of that shape. I have not turned towards a 'holistic' approach to the extent of losing interest in the history of the book's development, however; and I have tried to show how some themes prominent in the finished book do in fact go back, with whatever modifications, to the thought of Isaiah himself. Recent readings of Isaiah remind us—and this is timely—that the book exists now, in our own time, not just in the ancient world, and that we are entitled to put our own questions to it. It also reminds us that as a historical entity the book is probably a work of the Second Temple period, the fifth or fourth century BC, not of Isaiah's own century, the eighth. There is still room, however, for the recognition that some of the words the post-exilic compilers were arranging and editing really did originate in the eighth century; and there is room to be interested in the mind from which they sprang, the mind of one of the most creative thinkers in ancient Israel: Isaiah himself.

Further Reading

On unitary or holistic readings of biblical books, see

B.S. Childs, *Introduction to the Old Testament as Scripture* (Philadelphia: Fortress Press, 1979).

J.A. Sanders, *Torah and Canon* (Philadelphia: Fortress Press, 1972).

—*From Sacred Story to Sacred Text* (Philadelphia: Fortress Press, 1987).

*J.F.A. Sawyer, *From Moses to Patmos: New Perspectives in Old Testament Study* (London, 1977).

R. Alter and F. Kermode, *The Literary Guide to the Bible* (London: Collins, 1987); the article on Isaiah is by L. Alonso Schökel, pp. 165-83.

On holistic reading of Isaiah, see

E. W. Conrad, *Reading Isaiah* (Overtures to Biblical Theology, 27; Minneapolis: Fortress Press, 1991).

D. Carr, 'Reading for Unity in Isaiah', *JSOT* 57 (1993), pp. 61-80.

J.D.W. Watts, Isaiah 1–33 and *Isaiah 34–66* (WBC; Waco, TX: Word Books, 1985 and 1987).

W.L. Holladay, *Isaiah, Scroll of a Prophetic Heritage* (Grand Rapids: Eerdmans, 1978).

J.C. Exum, 'Isaiah 28–32: A Literary Approach', *SBLSP 1979* (vol. 2; Missoula, MT: Scholars Press, 1979), pp. 123-51.

C.R. Seitz, 'Isaiah 1–66: Making Sense of the Whole', *Reading and Preaching the Book of Isaiah* (ed. C.R. Seitz; Philadelphia: Fortress Press, 1988).

*W. Brueggemann, 'Unity and Dynamic in the Isaiah Tradition', *JSOT* 29 (1984), pp. 89-107.

R. Rendtorff, 'The Book of Isaiah: A Complex Unity: Synchronic and Diachronic Reading', *SBLSP 1991* (Atlanta: Scholars Press, 1991), pp. 8-20.

D.G. Johnson, *From Chaos to Restoration: An Integrative Reading of Isaiah 24–27* (JSOTSup, 61; Sheffield: JSOT Press, 1988).

M.A. Sweeney, 'The Book of Isaiah in Recent Research', in A.J. Hauser and P. Sellew (eds.), *Currents in Research: Biblical Studies*, I (Sheffield: JSOT Press, 1993), pp. 141-62.

On how the prophets were read in later times, see

J. Barton, *Oracles of God: Perceptions of Ancient Prophecy in Israel after the Exile* (London: Darton, Longman & Todd, 1986; New York: Oxford University Press, 1988), pp. 141-265.

M.A. Sweeney, *Isaiah 1–4 and the Post-Exilic Understanding of the Isaianic Tradition* (BZAW, 171; Berlin: de Gruyter, 1988).

On 'the Holy One of Israel', see

*D.P. Wright, 'Holiness', *ABD*, III, pp. 237-49.

On 'Israel', see

*L.L. Hoppe, 'Israel, History of, Monarchic Period', *ABD*, III, pp. 558-67.

On king, Messiah and Zion see

*M. de Jonge, 'Messiah', *ABD*, IV, pp. 777-88.

A. Laato, *Who is Immanuel? The Rise and Foundering of Isaiah's Messianic Expectations* (Åbo: Åbo Akademis Förlag, 1988).

*J.D. Levenson, 'Zion Traditions', *ABD*, VI, pp. 1098-1102.

On 'faith', see

*J.P. Healey, 'Faith (Old Testament)', *ABD*, II, pp. 744-49.

Also referred to

R. Murray, *The Cosmic Covenant* (London: Sheed & Ward, 1992), esp. pp. 14-26.

INDEXES

INDEX OF REFERENCES

INDEX OF AUTHORS